MW01272976

Car Trouble
True Stories from the Breakdown Lane
By Shawn Lake

Contents

Prologue

It's been a tough winch-out, with cables running up and downhill through pulleys strung from trees and dark closing in too fast. The road is icy here, where the tall Ponderosas have shaded it, and it's easy to see how the SUV got in trouble – the driver slowed down for the curve and gravity overpowered the forward momentum. The big vehicle slid to the lower edge of the road where it now sits, one wheel dangling over the edge. Just above on the road is a four-wheel-drive pickup whose owner stopped on this icy mountain road to help, then wisely gave up when his truck started sliding toward the SUV.

The two drivers are worried but playing it cool. They edge around on the ice, arms out for balance, angling for better views and offering advice as the tow truck driver hooks cables to frames, considers angles and thinks through possible outcomes. The vehicles' passengers are better behaved. They're doing their best to stay out of the way, though twice the Labrador retriever gets loose and bounds onto the ice.

Ken Field, the tow truck driver and engineer of the rescue, keeps his focus. He's used to dealing with personalities along with extraction strategies and he can work and talk at the same time. He's confident that his setup will work, and it does. The cables tighten, the wheels slide away from the edge, and the SUV pivots back onto the road. The pickup is easier – Ken drives it off the ice.

When everyone is back on safe ground, and Ken is doing the paperwork, one of the passengers – a young woman – comes over to shake his hand.

"You're awesome," she says.

On the way home, Ken pours some coffee from his thermos and laughs at that idea. I'm riding along because I happened to be at his house when the call came in, and because I'm writing about his job—the drama, the physics, the personalities and the business of towing.

Sometimes it's scary, sometimes it's funny and sometimes it is, in fact, awesome.

Ken started towing 35 years ago in Portland, Ore. He owned what he calls a "hillbilly backwoods" repair shop there, a business that was actually right downtown and served men and women in suits. Ken was getting along fine, sharing custody of his toddler, Nick, and playing drums on weekends. He'd have a beer now and then with his buddies after work, and if his life was a little low on joy, he was mercifully ignorant of the loss. Then he fell in love with the lead singer in his band, and everything changed.

And there you have the other side of this story about bad brakes, bad tires and bad luck. The singer was Tenley Holway, and when you met her a voice inside you said, "Wait. Her eyes are gold." She could build furniture and fell trees, repair just about anything, and sing *Angel from Montgomery* with enough heart to make John Prine smile.

Tenley and Ken got married and eventually left Ken's business and all the Portland music behind to start a new life in western Montana. She's in all of Ken's stories, even when she wasn't riding along. And later, when she got sick, the stories spiraled inward toward Tenley like comets falling to earth.

But now, after the night on the ice when Ken was awesome, Tenley's illness is a long ways down the road. Driving home in the dark, past the ghostly buildings of the Nine Mile Ranger Station and the dark shapes of the mules standing behind their fence, Ken talks about towing cars.

"It's a fine line," he says. "You have to appear to know exactly what you're doing, even while you're standing there trying to figure it out. They have to have confidence in me – their car is at the edge of disaster and I'm the one who is going to save it." Then he says, "But you don't want to be a jerk about it, either. A lot of guys get an exaggerated sense of their own importance."

I've seen Ken's technique before today, and I know that as soon as his feet hit the ground his clients feel better. He never makes them feel stupid or inadequate, even when they are. Instead, he sets a stage for them to write their own little play, one where they're all in it together and everyone gets to shake their heads at the unfairness of ice, leaky radiators, bad tires, and chance.

I've also seen enough recoveries to have formed some theories. I offer one to Ken as we bounce from the gravel road onto the pavement that winds down through the trees, and he shifts into fourth. The trees grow close to the road here, and we both keep a sharp eye out for deer.

"So this guy today, Steve. The first thing he did was to blame the whole thing on his wife," I say.

Ken thinks about it. "Well, sort of," he says.

"Then he told you how he'd towed tractors with ropes, and how good he is at fixing engines."

"Yeah," Ken says, but he isn't convinced. "He also ran the cable up the hill for me. And he found that pole to

4

use as a pry bar, did you see that? That truck wouldn't have swung around without him."

"Here's what I think," I say. "When a guy drives his car off the road and has to call for help, it puts him in a position of weakness. When another guy shows up to rescue him, that threatens his manhood. He can't react by getting mad or being a bully, because the car is still in trouble. So instead he jacks up his masculinity by trying to prove that he can do anything the wrecker driver can."

Ken gives me a look. He has a thin, craggy face, one you'd expect to see in a news photo of a climber just back from an ascent on some remote mountain. In his noisy tow truck with the heater on full blast, Ken is laughing at me. He likes my premise for its entertainment value, but he isn't buying it in the real world.

"OK, so now I suppose you're going to give me the Freudian interpretation," he says. "The vehicle is an extension of the male anatomy. They've lost it in the female abyss of the slushy road, and they want it back. I'm the big prick that shows up to save them, but what they really want to do is tell me to fuck off."

"Exactly!" I say, but I know my theory won't hold up. I've heard enough of Ken's tow stories to know that macho guys trying to prove themselves are boring compared to the real characters.

And that's what's in this book—the real characters. Ken's stories are no more than one degree of separation away from the event. That is, he told them to me and I'm telling them here. I was actually there for a few of them, but most are from Ken's remarkable memory. The characters are folks you might think you know. In fact, maybe you do. They're all real, and the stories are all true.

Which is not to say the words on these pages are exact. For example, what the Blackfeet Indian man named Eddie told Ken early one morning in a Helena parking lot may not be precisely recreated here. Ken's conversation with Tina from Arlee, on the other hand, is pretty much exactly word for word. But her name wasn't Tina.

In fact, many of the names are changed – sometimes to protect people from embarrassment, but usually because they are lost to memory. Names aren't important, but stories are meant to be told. There is no tow truck driver-client privilege, after all.

Chapter One •Driver Not On the Scene

Back in the early 1980s, when Ken was still fixing imported cars at Boulevard Motors in Portland, he drove a rickety Ford tow truck, part red and part black. It lifted cars with an electric boat winch mounted on its homemade bed.

Ken bought it from a guy who forgot to put antifreeze in the engine, and Ken glued the crack in the block with JB Weld. It was a truck that excelled around the Boulevard lot, jockeying cars out of the bays or into tight parking places. But like a criminal on home arrest, it was prohibited from doing any road work away from the property.

This was before Ken had done any real towing. It was before Tenley, and before he drove his Toyota into a tree and ended up in the hospital with head injuries. It was before fatherhood and responsibilities.

It was a time when Ken sometimes stopped off after work for a drink with friends, and this time he stayed too long. He remembers that he was drinking Spanish Coffees, a combination of hot coffee, heavy cream and rum, and that someone should have taken his keys at least an hour before he left. But they didn't, and Ken figured he'd just let his car find its own way home.

7

On this night, after a cold, drizzly Portland day, the car was a BMW. It was at the center of a deal that stood to make two of his customers at Boulevard Motors happy, and make Ken some money to boot.

"I had one guy who wanted to buy a BMW, and another guy who had one to sell," Ken told me some 25 years after the fact. Even then a look of hopeful enthusiasm crossed over his face, as if he could still make it happen. "It was a perfect deal."

The buyer, a Japanese businessman, was headed to Tokyo for three weeks. Since the little car needed work, a simple plan took shape for Ken.

"I got the money from Mr. Yamamoto, and I told him I'd have a Beamer ready when he came back. Then I bought the car from the other guy. Minus the cost of repairs, of course."

It was a shiny white model 2002, the classic BMW made from 1968 to 1976. These cars look almost the same front and back, with round headlights and tight, compact lines. "It didn't need a lot of work," said Ken. "I had it running in a week. It was kind of a hot rod."

He had to test drive it, of course, but the test soon became open ended as Ken started leaving his own car at home in favor of the Beamer. It was still registered to

8

the first owner, and the insurance issue was fuzzy. But the car was just too sweet to sit in the lot.

Then came the night of the Spanish Coffees. Dragging himself away from his friends, Ken left the bar and stood for a moment on the street before he got into the driver's seat. He knew he had to be careful, and he was. He stopped at every light, even the yellow ones, and waited an extra moment at stop signs to make sure. He made it all the way through downtown Portland, and by the time he'd left the city traffic behind he felt pretty good.

"I was almost home," he said. "I must have let my guard down."

Only a mile from his house, on a quiet street in a sleeping neighborhood, the little car drifted onto the shoulder, gravel popping under its tires, and Ken wasn't up to the challenge. In the slow-motion world of car accidents, the BMW plowed into the ditch, the steering wheel whipped around to break a bone in his hand, and the car rolled over on its side to rest among the fast-food wrappers and aluminum cans, radiator steaming and engine ticking in the night.

Ken climbed out and looked at the mess.

"I thought, 'Shit,'" he told me, from the vantage point of someone who has since towed hundreds of vehicles wrecked by drunken fools. The Japanese businessman flashed briefly before Ken's eyes, but he knew he had more immediate things to worry about. "I had to get that car out of there before someone showed up."

Holding his broken hand and fighting to clear his head, Ken jogged the mile down the road to his house.

"I got in my car and drove all the way downtown to the shop," Ken told me, still amazed. "I was very focused for someone who was still drunk. I just knew I had to get back before the cops showed up."

At the shop he unlocked the gate and climbed into the red Ford with the JB-Welded block, the truck that was only insured for use on the Boulevard lot. He drove back to the scene, maintaining a balance of excessively careful driving and repressed panic. Rounding the corner before his wreck, Ken's worst fears were realized – the scene was awash in flashing lights. His foot rose unbidden from the gas pedal.

"There were cops and fire trucks all over the place," said Ken. He can still feel the agony, but he laughs now as he covers his eyes with one arm. "It was too late. They'd seen me. I was driving a tow truck – I couldn't just pretend I was headed somewhere else."

When Ken pulled up at the scene an officer approached. He gave Ken a cautious look.

"Are you from Buck's towing?" he asked.

And there it was. The moment of miraculous opportunity. Ken took it.

"Yep," he said, and drove down into the ditch.

Looking past Ken now, out his living room window at Nine Mile, Montana, I can see two wrecked vehicles – recent customers. One was a highway roll-over, and the other was a pickup that slid off a mountain road with the bed piled high with firewood. The pickup had been a tricky recovery, and Ken had to set up his truck and cables three different times to get it out. But that night in Portland, he had never before extracted a wreck. He looked at the little BMW, and he knew that speed was his only friend.

"I hooked two chains on wherever I could find a place and jumped into the wrecker. I knew they were all watching, but all I could think of was to get out of there. I winched it over and it goes, 'whump,' back onto the wheels."

That's when the last of his confidence leaked away. He romped on the gas and popped the little car out of the ditch and took off down the road.

"It's all bent up and the frame's dragging on the road," Ken told me from the safety of years. "No glass,

11

tires all flat. I didn't even lift it into the air. I just hit the gas and took off. There were chains dragging and metal scraping the pavement. I looked into the rear view mirror and all those cops were watching, and there's a rooster tail of sparks behind me. I just kept going."

And he made it. It was just a mile, after all, and after he pulled into his yard and checked to see that the little car wouldn't catch fire in front of his house, he went inside and sat down. His head was spinning and his hand hurt, and he thought he might throw up. He knew that he'd have to refund the money to the Japanese businessman, and deal with insurance claims and medical bills. And he also knew that back down the road, amid the flashing lights, another tow truck was surely pulling up. The cops certainly said to him, "Hey, one of your guys was already here. And boy, what an idiot."

In the elegant circle of events that gives hope that there is meaning to life, Ken was in another bar years later when a couple of guys came in wearing Buck's Towing hats. He didn't hesitate to buy them a beer.

"I've got to tell you a story," he said, and he did. It didn't take long for them to look at each other and laugh.

"That was us," one of the Buck's guys said. "We always wondered who the hell that guy was."

Chapter Two • The Squeaky Wheel

Tenley Holway was on a ladder in her front yard, painting her house yellow, when the new guy showed up to apply for the drummer job. It was a warm Portland Saturday, and she was enjoying the sun on her shoulders when she heard the distinctive sound of a Volkswagen bus behind her. She had a weakness for VW buses.

The guy was Ken. Tall and skinny, faded jeans and tee shirt, long hair in a ponytail, he had a kind of loose-limbed grace. He angled his head to one side and smiled as though he already knew her. His eyes had a sparkle like sun through a glass of water.

"I'm the drummer," he said.

Tenley put down her brush. "I can audition you," she said.

What she thought was, *You've got the job*.

When they told me this story, in their living room on Nine Mile Hill in Montana fifteen years later, Ken and Tenley took turns talking, laughing and correcting details. When Tenley told me she'd been "smitten" with Ken from the start, he grinned. He was strumming an Epiphone Serenader twelve-string, and Tenley stopped talking to listen to a riff. They'd just returned from the National Oldtime Fiddlers Contest in Weiser, Idaho, where they took a workshop in swing guitar.

"I don't remember that one," she said. She reached for her Martin. "Do it again," she said.

Back in 1989, in Portland, Ken did get the job. He started playing with Cayuse, at the back of the stage with his drums while Tenley played her guitar at the front. The lead guitar player was her boyfriend, but Ken couldn't stop watching her as she sang.

***

Like most musicians, Ken kept his day job. His funky auto repair shop in downtown Portland had a high-end clientele of doctors, lawyers and hip businessmen. They liked Boulevard Motors because it provided a quirky contrast to the glass and chrome businesses that charged $1500 to replace a water pump. Ken and his partner, a Polish immigrant whose name translated as Richard, joked with their customers and gave them stories to take back to the office.

Boulevard Motors was a converted gas station, with a glass front and two bays. It had the requisite V-belts hanging along the wall, the shelves of gaskets and rags, and the red, five-drawer tool cases on wheels. Ken and

Richard built the business themselves, and both of them liked their work.

Ken liked his work even when he'd played a gig until late the night before. But one Saturday morning it seemed nothing would go right, and when he straightened his aching back and stared gloomily at the green antifreeze dripping from a radiator hose onto the floor, his head pounded. He pushed the hair out of his eyes with the back of his hand, streaking his forehead with black grease, and considered going to lunch before he took the Saab 900's water pump off again. It was a new pump, but every time he tightened the bolts and started the car, it leaked. The car's owner, a doctor at Oregon Health & Science University, had made it clear she needed the car the next day.

Now Ken put socket to bolt for the third time, reminding himself with every turn that Saab made these particular bolts with left-hand threads. Right was not tight, and left was not loose. He placed each bolt in a box at his feet.

He was on the last one when he heard a voice he'd hoped to forget.

"Ken?" whined the man, speaking to Ken's back without waiting for an answer. "I was putting the new thingies on the brakes, and I didn't have the right tools.

You know that tool you need to put those thingies in? So I was wondering if you'd mind checking them for me?" His voice rose at the end of his sentences, turning every statement into an irritating question.

Ken didn't have to look to know who it was. Bob had brought his 280Z to the shop not long before, and Ken put in a turbo-charged engine for him. Bob was a pest through the whole process – he called every day and then made excuses to come by anyway, slinking around the waiting room or worming his way into the back to poke around in the tool drawers and look over Ken's shoulder. Ken had pointed out that the car needed other work more than it needed an engine – the body was rusty and dented, the windshield cracked, the brakes squealed.

"Yeah, but Ken?" Bob had said then. "Can you have the engine in by Friday?"

Now Ken sighed and turned around, crossing his arms. Bob was standing in the door between the office and the shop, shifting his weight from foot to foot. He was no more than five feet four, and his thin brown hair was slicked straight back from his forehead. He looked about Ken's age, mid-thirties, but he fidgeted like a kid on the playground, pushing hard to get picked for the team.

And now he was fixing his own brakes.

"Hello, Bob," Ken said evenly. "How's the engine running?"

"It runs great, Ken," said Bob. "You wouldn't believe how fast it is."

Ken could believe it. He'd driven it. "That's great, Bob. Leave it out front and I'll take a look at the brakes as soon as I can." He turned back to the Saab – one more bolt and then he could pull the pump, check the gaskets again. Maybe it was the seals inside the pump, a long shot, but not impossible. Underneath his calculations about the Saab, he was trying to think of Bob's last name, which he remembered was significant in some way.

Bob sidled through the door and into the bay. He dismissed the Saab with a glance, and went on as though Ken hadn't spoken. "You know how those thingies have to hook back in? And it's really hard to do it without that tool." He made prying motions with his hands. "I think I got it, but if you could just check."

Ken closed his eyes for a moment, then set the wrench down on his rag on the fender. He took a deep breath and turned to talk to Bob, and the wrench slipped off and clattered to the floor.

"Listen, Bob," Ken said. "Can you give me a minute here? Go sit in the waiting room and I'll be right out."

"OK, Ken, but can I have it back before lunch?"

Ken picked up his wrench and looked at Bob. The guy always wore some kind of loud shirt, and today it was Hawaiian. He'd just remembered Bob's last name. It was Weiner. Rhymes with whiner. Ken's partner Richard had worked the name over when they were putting in his engine, during the few hours Bob had been absent from the shop.

"This is a man with a warning label," Richard had said then, his Polish accent giving weight to his words.

Now Ken turned away from Bob Weiner without answering, hoping to just get the last bolt out of the Saab's water pump so he could clear his mind. He slipped the socket back over the bolt and fit the ratchet into it.

Bob made it to the waiting room door and then turned. "Oh, and Ken? It's also making this funny noise." he whined. "I don't know if it's the brakes, but there's this noise."

Ken felt Bob's voice climb up his back and he growled to himself as he cranked the bolt. When it resisted he gave it just a little more, and at the moment

18

he felt it finally give he knew what he'd done. The bolt snapped off with a dull chunk. He'd been tightening instead of loosening.

Ken didn't move for a moment. He looked at the bolt head inside the socket, and at the rough broken edge of the other half still in the engine block, and he knew he'd have to spend the next two days pulling the engine, drilling and tapping the bolt hole, and putting the engine back in. And he still didn't know if the water pump would leak.

He turned to face Bob. "Where's the car, Bob?" he asked in a flat, controlled voice. Bob brightened, happy now that he had Ken's attention. He motioned through the doorway to the big window, where the battered Datsun sat directly in front of the shop.

"It's right there, Ken. Here's the keys." He dropped the keys in Ken's hand and left, turning back at the door. "And Ken? I eat lunch at noon."

Ken didn't rush into the 280Z. He fixed the Saab, which cost him an extra day's work and an unhappy customer. He went on to a few other jobs, and even took a day off. But every time he looked out the front window, there was that car. The little black Datsun, that had once seemed zippy and cool, now invoked car crushers and scrap metal. Looking at it brought Bob Weiner's voice to

Ken's ear. "Those thingies Ken? You know the ones?" Ken would shudder and go find something else to do.

Then one day he needed to pick up a part at Riviera Motors, in downtown Portland. He started to hop into his Toyota, but right next to it sat the 280Z. The car reeked of misery and failure, but Ken knew if he just drove it one time, listened to Bob's noise, he could get rid of it. Then he remembered the turbo engine he'd put in.

Ken grabbed the keys from the rack and slid behind the wheel.

In a better world, Ken wouldn't have been in a hurry to get to Riviera Motors. He wouldn't have let himself be seduced by the fast ride he knew he'd get from the Z. He would have remembered what an airhead Bob was, and put the car on the lift before he drove it.

What actually happened was that he tapped the pedal as he rolled out of the lot and found that he had enough brakes to stop. Fueled by his irritation at Bob, he took off down the road and cranked it up to sixty right off. He did hear a little noise so he rolled down the window to listen, and then he ran it up to seventy. It was probably the front brake calipers that Bob hooked up wrong.

It was a beautiful day, and Ken put his elbow out the window. The wind came in, whipping his hair into his eyes, and he took a deep breath and smiled. He felt an odd little wobble in the front end, but it only lasted a few seconds.

Then Ken saw something black streak down the road in front of him. He had a moment of detached curiosity before he realized the object was his left front wheel.

Suddenly released from the weight of the car, the wheel sailed down Front Avenue through traffic. Cars swerved and braked as it flew between them, somehow avoiding each speeding vehicle.

The Z hung suspended as Ken watched the tire, his foot still on the gas. The rear-wheel drive car ran smoothly now that it was free of the wobbling wheel, and Ken had just enough time to think, "Oh my god," before he lifted his foot from the gas and the car, without forward momentum, slammed down on the hub. Sparks climbed over the hood as he fought with the steering, and through the fireworks he watched brake lights flash as the wheel disappeared in front of a lane of cars.

By the time Richard got there in the tow truck, Ken had waved on a dozen kind citizens, picked up pieces of brake rotor from a hundred yards of pavement, and paced around the crippled 280Z enough times to wear a path. All the while listening to Bob Weiner's voice in his head.

"He didn't tighten the lug nuts," said Richard before he even got out of the tow truck, and Ken nodded. Richard backed up to the Z with Ken walking alongside next to the driver's window.

"How basic is that?" Ken said. From the moment Bob Weiner had first walked into their shop, he'd scrambled Ken's judgment. All his mechanic's instincts had been sabotaged by the aura of nervous energy that surrounded the man.

Richard hopped down and looked at the car. The hub was ground flat on one side and the tie rods were chewed up. Brake lines and various cables hung in the wheel well like the legs of a dead spider.

Richard's eyes followed the gouge in the pavement that led from the hub back up Front Avenue. Then he turned the other way. "Where is the wheel?"

Ken waved on another car that had slowed to stare at the Z, hunched over its ruined hub. He nodded down the avenue. "That way," he said.

They winched the car up to the tow truck and merged into traffic, heading after the wheel with the Willamette River on their right and the city of Portland on their left. Strips of rubber from disintegrated retreads caught their eyes, along with black plastic trash bags and an abandoned tire – that wasn't on a wheel. Ken quit looking after a quarter mile, glad he hadn't seen a multi-car pileup with a Datsun wheel at the center. He sat miserably with one foot on the dash board as they neared Riviera Motors.

"Might as well pick up that alternator," he said.

A half-mile later Richard started to pull over, but their turn was still a few blocks away. Ken looked at him, and then followed his gaze to some bushes alongside the road as they rolled to a stop. There was a fourteen-inch tire, on a wheel. The bolt holes in the wheel were burred and jagged, beaten into irregular ovals by the Datsun's lugs. Unlike its owner, the wheel from Bob Weiner's car had traveled a remarkable path past a multitude of people without causing damage. Ken stood over it for a moment before he shook his head, picked it up and threw it on the back of the wrecker.

Chapter Three • Drop-Ins Welcome

Boulevard Motors was a cult favorite among the affluent, high-end British car owners in Portland. Customers loved the funky old gas station motif, and Midas Muffler had even shot a commercial there. In the commercial, Boulevard's cluttered office served as the dark side of the muffler business, a pointed contrast to Midas' tidy shop. A ratty, B-movie guy sat in Ken's chair with his feet up on the desk, stubby cigar in his mouth. The unspoken message was, "Are you going to trust your car to this guy?"

The real customers did trust their cars to Boulevard. But occasionally someone would show up who tried Ken's patience, or even his credulity. One of them was a cheerful, wiry woman driving a vintage Ford sedan.

"It was a '49 or '50, the kind with the big chrome bullet in the grille," said Ken. "It was mint – all shined up, lowered, a real hot rod."

But an overheated hot rod. The woman screeched into the lot and slid to a stop, steam boiling from under her hood. She got out, threw her cigarette on the pavement and ground it out with her boot. When Ken came out, she grinned at him like an old friend.

"Hey," she said. "Got any water?" She had tattoos on her biceps and a short, spiky haircut, but everything about her body language was open and friendly. Ken could have been her buddy from the classic Ford club, along for the ride.

Ken got the hose, and when he got back she had the hood up. The engine was ticking and crackling like a pot on the stove, and he started to warn her about taking the radiator cap off while it was still so hot. He needn't have worried.

Taking the hose, she unscrewed the oil filler cap instead, and shoved the hose in. Then she looked up and Ken and smiled. "Bitchin' hot day, huh?" she said.

Ken was speechless as water gushed back out the hole. By the time he found his voice, water was spewing from the valve cover as well, and spreading over the lot in an oily pond.

"No, no, wait, don't do that!" he said, reaching his hand toward the Ford. "That's where the oil goes."

"Ah, I do it all the time," she said, and threw down the hose. "Cools it right down."

There was nothing left to say as the woman screwed the cap back on and slammed the hood. She gave Ken a quick salute goodbye from the driver's seat, then cranked the key.

"Hey, thanks a lot," she said, and dropped it into gear. Steam streaked from under her hood as she burned rubber out onto Barbur Boulevard, and disappeared in a cloud of smoke.

***

Another woman, this one in a 930 Porsche, was the polar opposite of the hot rod lady. Elegant and graceful without even getting out of the car, she buzzed down her window and offered Ken her beautiful but troubled smile. Her windshield wipers weren't working. It was pouring rain. Could he please try to help her out?

Ken had pulled a jacket over his head to run out to the car when she pulled in the lot, and now he edged it up over his head. It was raining so hard the shop was a gray outline behind him, and only her headlights had alerted him that a car was outside. He'd been taking a break, looking out the big front windows, and when he saw it was a Porsche he decided to see what was up. Now raindrops were splashing onto the woman's shoulder, spotting the silk jacket, and Ken felt compelled to save her from any inconvenience. He looked into the space between the windshield and the hood where the wiper mechanism sits.

"Turn them on for a minute," he said.

The blade on the passenger side swept smoothly over the perfect glass, but the one on the driver's side just jerked in ineffective spasms. Ken could see where part of the linkage had become disconnected.

"Hold on a minute, I'll get a wrench," he said.

She smiled again and buzzed her window back up. Her hands on the steering wheel were manicured and her diamond rings were artfully simple. This was a woman who knew how to accept favors.

Ken ran to the shop and grabbed a 13 millimeter wrench, then trotted back out to the Porsche. When he leaned over to reach for the linkage, he couldn't help seeing the woman's legs in shiny stockings, a modest few inches of knee visible at the edge of her skirt. She had folded her hands in her lap as she waited. She could have been on her way to a charity ball or an opera, nearly late now with this worrisome delay.

Ken had already decided he wouldn't charge her. The goodwill would be more valuable than a few bucks.

"OK, try it again," he said, peering at the linkage, which worked like the huge wheels and connecting rods on an old locomotive—in this case transmitting the motion from a little wheel to the sweep of the wiper arm.

Ken's mind may have been still on the shiny stockings when the motor started, catching his finger in the mechanism. It was like a kid's nightmare monster, grabbing his arm and pulling him into the dark, and it didn't let go as Ken's face smacked into the windshield. In the moment of surprise before he could speak, he saw her eyes through the glass, widening in horror.

"Turn it off!" he yelled. "Turn it off!" His face was pushed into the wet glass, mouth and nose distorted and grotesque in pain as the wiper arms stroked relentlessly back and forth, dragging Ken's face along with them.

Inches away, the woman was frozen in shock for a few seconds, then she began a choked, frantic whimpering. Through the glass and muted by the rain, the sound came to Ken as though from a great distance, enforcing the nightmare quality of his predicament. He yelled louder for her to shut off the wipers, but she seemed stunned and pressed herself back in the seat.

Finally, she released her grip from the wheel long enough to turn the switch off, then grabbed the wheel again. She was quiet now, but her eyes were wide. Ken leaned away from the glass and untangled his hand from the wiper mechanism, breathing hard. Blood dripped from a ragged cut on his finger. From inside the car the rain-and-blood-streaked window framed the woman's view: a stranger turning his bloody hand to her, wet strands of hair stuck to his face and an expression of shock still pulling at his features.

She started the car.

Ken backed away and tried to speak, but the pain stopped him. He didn't know how badly he was hurt, and he also didn't know if he'd fixed the wiper. He leaned over to look in her window.

"Lady?" he said loudly, over the rain and the engine. He was still holding his bleeding hand up. "You should try them again."

The woman's manners wouldn't let her drive away, but she couldn't look at Ken. Staring straight ahead, she winced as she spoke through the closed side window. "Please, don't try anything else. I just want to leave."

In truth, that was fine with Ken, too. He stood for just a moment watching her pull into traffic, wiper blades slapping evenly, before he trotted through the rain back to the shop.

***

The hot rod lady and the wiper blade woman each had redeeming features. Neither was pushy or demanding, and each seemed like someone he could have had a conversation with under different circumstances.

This could not be said of the woman in the white VW Rabbit who needed directions. It was another rainy day, but this time Ken was busy. He'd had a series of frustrating jobs that morning, and when he heard her honking he tried to ignore it. But the sound pierced through the rain and the walls and into Ken's weary consciousness. He set down his tools, wiped his hands, and went outside.

The woman rolled down her window just enough to speak through the crack. She was wearing a white fur coat, and she gave Ken a thin smile that quickly faded into a frown. She was tapping one hand impatiently on the wheel.

"Can you tell me how to get to Barbur Boulevard?" she said.

Ken hesitated. Over the top of the Rabbit he could see the street sign that said Barbur Boulevard. His shop was named for the wide, four-lane street out front. It would have been easy to just point to Barbur and say, "It's right there," and go back inside. But sometimes the easiest way isn't the most satisfying way. The rain dripped from the hood on Ken's rain jacket as he smiled to himself.

"OK," he said to the woman. Pointing toward the sign for Interstate 5, he said, "You get on the freeway south and go down to the Tigard exit. Get off there, and go to 217. Stay on 217 until you get to the exit for Highway 26, and take that until you see the sign for the zoo. Get off there, and follow the signs to downtown. And you'll be right on Barbur."

The woman was still frowning, trying to remember it all, but at the end she looked relieved. She rolled her window up, pinching off her distracted thank you, and drove to the edge of the lot where she waited to merge into traffic.

Ken watched from inside the shop, searching for a pang of remorse. There was none.

***

Another time, it was Ken's partner Richard who had no remorse. He and Ken were bent over an engine when a customer came in asking about a deck lid for a '65 VW Beatle. The customer was a weasely guy with thinning hair in an anemic ponytail.

Ken had acquired just such a deck lid in a trade a while back. This guy must have heard about it from someone in the used-parts loop.

"Blaine," he introduced himself, holding out his hand to Ken. "And you're...?"

Ken told him and shook his hand. He didn't get a good feeling from the guy, but he'd be happy to sell him the deck lid. "Yeah, I've got one in the back."

"Nice shop you have here, Ken" said Blaine.

Ken thought, Eddie Haskell. He wondered if Blaine would also compliment him on his fine work shirt. He went into the back room to look for the deck lid.

It took Ken a few minutes to find it where it leaned against a wall, behind an old welder and draped with a pair of dirty coveralls. He pulled it out and gave it a few whacks with the coveralls to displace the dust, then he carried it out into the waiting room and propped it against the counter.

Blaine looked at the deck lid in silence for a moment, then pulled himself to his full height and circled it like a cop at a crime scene. He frowned and shook his head.

"I don't know, Ken. The paint's a little bubbled here," he said, pointing. "Could be rust underneath."

"Could be," Ken said.

Blaine put his hands in his pockets. "How much do you want for it?" he said.

"Thirty bucks."

Thirty dollars was cheap, but Blaine frowned. He leaned forward and turned the handle. It squeaked.

"Hmm," he said. "Kind of rough."

Richard was now leaning in the doorway, and Ken saw him smile. Richard was as tall as Ken, but built like an oak tree. If not for his blue work shirt with his name on the pocket, he could have been heaving kegs of beer up onto a mule-drawn wagon, then driving the team off down the cobbled street.

"WD-40," Ken said.

"How about ten?" asked Blaine, his eyes on the deck lid.

Ken looked at him for a moment, then went into the office and picked up the telephone. While he was gone, Richard stayed in the doorway. Blaine didn't look at him.

"Columbia gets fifty for theirs," said Ken when he came back.

"But you know what, Ken?" said Blaine, turning to face him. "I'm going to have to get it painted. That's going to cost me."

Ken shook his head in exasperation. "OK, listen. Give me twenty bucks."

"I really think ten is fair, Ken."

Ken rubbed his eyes, starting to think he should let it go for ten just to get Blaine out of his shop. He started to speak, but Richard interrupted.

"Excuse me," he said from the doorway, pushing his accent toward eastern-European bad guy. "Perhaps you would like to have this deck lid for free?"

Blaine's eyebrows went up. "Free?" he asked.

Richard walked over to the deck lid and tipped it away from the counter. He balanced it with his hand. "For free, yes."

Blaine looked at Ken for a clue, but Ken's face was blank. Blaine said. "Well, yeah. I guess that would be fine."

"OK, good," said Richard. He laid the deck lid down, raised his booted foot and brought it down hard. Then he stomped again and again until the paint splintered and the little handle broke off. Then he got on top of it and jumped until the gentle curve that once had completed the lines of a classic bug was almost flat.

Blaine had backed away at the first stomp, and now he stood open mouthed and speechless. He tore his eyes away from the ruined deck lid and looked at Ken. Ken smiled and shrugged.

34

Finally Richard stepped back onto the floor and nodded at Blaine.

"There, for free," he said. "Have a nice day."

Chapter Four • For Better or Worse

A few days before Christmas, 1990, Ken woke up earlier than usual, and opened his eyes to a panorama of sparkling lights. He wondered how the decorations had gotten into the bedroom, then realized that the lights were inside his head. He closed his eyes and thought, *It's time to go back to the hospital.*

It started the week before, in the early morning hours after a gig. Ken was driving his Toyota home through a light snow, going slowly because he was tired and the road was icy and Tenley was following in the VW bus. It shouldn't have been a bad accident, just a slow motion skid into a tree. But he wasn't wearing a seat belt, and when his head hit the windshield he left an imprint of his face in the glass.

The hospital sent him home that night, but he was back in a few days with a bad headache. This time they kept him for two days before releasing him with warnings about dizziness and pain. Ken didn't like being in the hospital and he was glad to go home.

Then came the dancing lights, and when Ken realized he'd have to go back to the hospital he broke down and cried. He had things to do – his job, his music, his toddler Nick.

But there was no doubt Ken was very sick. A subdural hematoma was pressing on his brain, and for the next two weeks he went in and out of consciousness in the hospital bed. When he wasn't unconscious, he was scared.

"They kept doing MRIs, and the hematoma was getting bigger," Ken told me. "I was hours away from brain surgery, and I really didn't want to do that." Then the doctors took one more MRI. The swelling had gone down, and the door to the operating room swung shut.

When Ken finally went home, Christmas and New Years were over and the gray, drizzly Portland winter was well under way. But there was a bright spot: Tenley. She took care of his house while he was gone and spent every day with him at the hospital. When he came home, she stayed.

Ken's head injury wasn't the first bad luck he and Tenley had. A few years before they met, two thugs in ski masks kicked in Ken's front door while he was watching Johnny Carson on TV. They kicked him in the head and ransacked the house, taking his wallet and picking up his Epiphone like it was a stick of wood. Ken watched, semi-conscious as the two tipped over furniture and pulled out drawers, stopping only to plant another kick into Ken's back as they passed. But when they tried to tie his hands behind his back, he knew he had to act.

"They rolled me over on my stomach and got out a piece of rope, and I flipped out," Ken says. "There were two of them, but they were just little guys.

But they did have a sawed-off shotgun. Ken wrenched free and got one of them in a head lock, running on anger and adrenaline. The punk managed to scream, "Kill him," and his buddy fired the shotgun into the floor before he broke for the door. Ken released his hold and in a second they were both gone. Miraculously, the Epiphone was leaning unharmed by the door.

Tenley's brush with death came at work, while she was helping an older couple pick out wallpaper at the Standard Brands hardware store where she worked. She said "Hi" to the two guys when they came through the door, but they barely glanced at her on their way to the customer service desk. Tenley was leafing through pastel floral patterns in the wallpaper book when she heard the pop.

"I knew it was a gun shot," Tenley told me. "I told my customers to get out of there, and they did."

Meanwhile the robbers shoved two sales clerks to the floor, fired a shot through the hand of the customer service manager, and grabbed some money. They came running back the way they'd come, right past Tenley.

"They came around the corner and saw me. One of them grabbed me by my hair and said, 'You're coming with us.' But I couldn't walk."

It had turned into one of those dreams scenes, where your arms and legs won't work. The robber shoved Tenley to her knees and she studied his sneakers as he fumbled with his pistol. She could hear it, the sound of metal clicking and sliding over metal. She felt his hand pull her hair tighter and then she heard something hit the floor. An empty shell rolled to rest near the robber's feet.

"I knew I was dead," says Tenley. "I'd looked him right in the face, he knew I could identify him."

But after a while, the robber just walked away and left her. The two were never caught.

Ken and Tenley's close calls came years before they met, but they both had friends with similar stories. "Everyone we knew had some kind of experience with violence or crime," Ken told me. "It was bad."

As bad as it was, though, they might have stuck it out. Between them, Ken and Tenley had three young kids. Both their extended families lived in Portland, and the music was there. Ken had Boulevard Motors, and in the year after Tenley moved in she made the house in Gabriel Park into a home. She landscaped the yard, added paint, wallpaper and carpet. They had even added an extra bedroom and bathroom for the kids.

And therein lay the problem. The kids were the ones they worried about, not only their safety but their futures. Just sending them to school was like watching them walk a tight rope over a shark tank every day, and finally Ken and Tenley knew they had to find another way.

When they started looking for a new place to live, they thought first of Montana. They had a friend in a place called Nine Mile.

Chapter Five • Nine Mile Auto Wreakers

The first time Ken and Tenley drove by their future home, they laughed. They had driven over from Portland to visit their friend Mark, who lived down the road, and they pulled over at the top of the hill to take a look. An empty, one-room general store sat behind a gas island that hadn't seen pumps since the 1970s, and next to that was a dingy garage with a sign dangling from one hinge. The sign read, "Nine Mile Auto Wreakers."

Behind the store was a vacant double-wide, with dirty windows and a shed out back that still held a few chicken feathers. The saving grace was the stand of tall Ponderosa pines that surrounded the little cluster of buildings, and the field of grass that rose up the hill to the east to meet a rim of trees. Interstate 90 lay just over the hill to the north, and the cliffs that rose on the other side of the Clark Fork River were visible to the south.

Ken laughed, but he saw possibilities.

When they got back to Portland, he got busy. He went to the library and made phone calls, and found the place was owned by a man named Phil Cyr. Ken eventually learned that Phil owned hundreds of acres there at one time, and had run cattle and raised his family there. A campground and gas station entered the picture at some point, but finally the land started to go, piece by piece. Ken learned that Phil managed to keep the old store at the top of the hill, along with the garage, the doublewide and a few acres. He lived in a house down the road with his wife. It was almost a cliché, but it touched Ken. He felt a connection to the place from the start. He wrote Phil a letter.

"I told him I really liked the place, and if he ever decided to sell he should call me," says Ken.

And in November of 1993, he did.

They had a talk. It turned out Phil had rented the place out a number of times, and had even sold it before. The best of the tenants just ran out of money. The worst cheated customers on car repairs and got in feuds with the neighbors. The last one left the garage full of old Cadillac parts and unidentifiable railroad equipment. So Phil was cautious.

But winter was coming, and he didn't want to leave the place empty. And he and Ken got along. They made a deal.

The only concession Phil wanted was to keep some of the land.

"I used to own all of this," he told Ken. "I'd kind of like to keep some of it." Phil kept the seven-acre field that rises up a gentle slope just east of the buildings. He sold the rest to Ken.

Chapter Six • Indian Affairs

When the knocking at Ken's door finally penetrated his sleep, he'd only been in bed less than an hour. It was 11:00 p.m. on a winter night, and when he looked out his window Ken saw a black Camaro in his driveway. He didn't want to deal with it.

But that first year in Montana was tough. Nine Mile Auto Wreakers became Nine Mile Auto Repair, and it brought in a few bucks. But insurance on the tow truck was $1500 a year, a lot in those days. And then there were the payments on the truck, and the mortgage, and all the other expenses of just getting by. So Ken dragged himself out of bed. When he saw who it was, he regretted it.

"I was a little worried," Ken told me later.

By the time I heard this story, Ken had lived in Montana for ten years. He was the tow service of choice for the locals, and was juggling car deals with wrecking yards and car traders from Hamilton to Hot Springs. He and Tenley were also deep into the western Montana music culture, playing in bands for weddings and parties, and jamming in the little local taverns where the guy on

44

the next bar stool goes home to get his Dobro when the music starts.

But back then, Ken was a newcomer from the city. And the two big Blackfeet Indian men on his porch made him nervous.

Under his yard light, Ken could see more people in the car, cigarette tips glowing. "It was awful," Ken told me. "I was profiling. I hate that. But my wife and kids were asleep in the house." Memories of guns and bad guys in Portland were still fresh. The Montana night was peaceful and quiet, but Ken was still on guard.

Then one of the men spoke, in the measured, softly graceful inflection of Native American English.

"Hey, man. How's it going?" It sounded as if he really wanted to know.

"Well, it's going OK, I guess," said Ken. "I'll bet it's not with you, though."

Both men laughed. The second guy looked toward the Camaro. "This is about as far as we're going to make it. The headlights are so dim they're, like, brown."

"Alternator?" Ken asked. It sounded like they'd been running on their battery, a limited proposition at best.

"Yeah," said the first man. "Since about St. Regis. I can't believe we made it this far."

Ken hesitated. These guys weren't full of chatter, which was a relief. A lot of late night callers buzz with the need to justify their visit, rattling on about the history of their car trouble all the way back to when they bought it. These two just looked at him evenly.

Stalling for time, Ken looked at the Camaro and said, "How many people you got in there?"

"Two."

The cold air was leaking through the open door. "I can't fix it tonight," Ken said.

"No, all we need is a tow. I got a friend in Missoula, he's got an alternator that will work."

Ken hesitated. He looked past the men over at Phil's field, just east of his house. No deer tonight, but it looked serene and lovely just the same. You couldn't tell that Interstate 90 lay just over the hill.

Ken turned back to the two guys on the porch, who were watching him quietly, and he decided to go for it. He hooked up the Camaro, crammed the two men and two kids into the cab of the wrecker, and headed east.

In the winter in Montana, weeks sometimes go by without sun. But there are also bright days when you can't look at the snow without sunglasses, and sharp, cold nights with more stars than sky. It was one of those nights as Ken and his crew rolled down the highway, the white guy crammed against his door and the Natives sitting on each other's laps between him and the other door. It may have been their unembarrassed intimacy, arms around shoulders and knees against the dash, that reassured Ken.

"I'm a pretty good judge of character," he told me. "These guys were scary looking, but they were all right." They had craggy, serious faces and long black hair in braids, some were missing teeth though they were all under forty. They wore ragged jeans, which are pretty much a uniform in western Montana, but one had a fine, beaded belt. One kid was wearing a Salish-Kootenai College sweatshirt. Ken pried his arm out of the crush and offered it for a shake.

"I'm Ken, by the way," he said.

Next to him was the big guy from the porch. He seemed to be the leader. "I'm Eddie," he said, and managed to shake Ken's hand. The next guy over said, "My name is Eddie, too." Then he said, as though it was an explanation, "I'm his cousin."

That got a little more of a laugh than Ken thought it warranted, until he shook hands with Chris and then another Eddie. The kid gave it a beat and then said, "Cousin," and everyone laughed again.

Having three Eddies in his tow truck convinced Ken that he'd made the right choice. The Camaro was towing smoothly, there was no traffic, and the wrecker was running fine. It was only twenty miles to the Wye, a cluster of truck stops, bars and motels at the intersection of I-90 and US Highway 93. Ken would drop them off there, they would call their friend with the alternator, and Ken would collect his money and go home.

At the Crossroads Travel Center, the first Eddie went in to make a call. It turned out to be a number of calls, and the whole crew ended up in the coffee shop, looking at the racks of cassette tapes and buying pop and candy bars. The kids stayed close to the adults and didn't whine. They used the men's room when it was their turn. After a while Eddie got off the phone.

"Hey, man," he said to Ken. "How much to tow that thing to Helena?"

By this time the wheel of fortune was starting to point toward the Indians. Ken liked the whole, frayed bunch of them, and though he was still cautious he felt a little like a goodwill ambassador from white America.

"They were in dire straits," he told me. "They had just been to a powwow and spent all their money. They had little kids with them. Their car was dying and they couldn't get hold of the guy with the alternator. And they were all cheerful."

But Ken had a dilemma. He had to trust that they'd pay him when they got there, which would be about 3:00 a.m. He had to trust that everything would go well with the tow, and he had to figure out how much to charge. Since he didn't know how far it was to Helena, he made it up. "A hundred-fifty, and you pay the gas," he told them.

Eddie said OK, as though he were accepting another cup of coffee, and they all climbed back in the truck. Back on the highway, it was like they were on their way to a family gathering. Vastly outnumbered and in a good mood, Ken let them rag him.

Chris had a tomahawk he got at the powwow, and he angled it toward Ken. "Hey Eddie," he said. "What do you think?"

"I don't know, man," Eddie said. "He's driving."

"But look at his hair, Man," Chris said. "It would look so good on my belt."

"No, no," Ken protested. "I'm one of the good guys. I've got my white hat here somewhere." Then, "Oh, wait. That's a cowboy thing, isn't it."

"Go ahead and scalp him."

Ken cringed in mock terror, and they all laughed. It was really a peace offering, this joking around; a sign that they liked him enough to tease him a little. They told him about car wrecks they'd had, other white guys they'd scared. When they said that they all quit drinking, Ken gave them a look. It could be true, he thought.

After fifty miles, Ken realized he'd made a miscalculation. His full tank of gas had dropped to below a quarter, and though he'd never been to Helena before he knew they still had to cross six-thousand-foot MacDonald Pass. In the full moon the hills along Highway 90 looked strangely barren, the pines scrubby and deformed compared to the ones near Nine Mile. Ken didn't want to wind up out of gas at the side of that road

When they rolled into Garrison Junction, where Montana Highway 12 left the interstate, Ken's heart sank. The gas station was closed. Sitting in the lot, with the engine ticking as it cooled, Ken turned to Eddie.

"I know this truck," he said. "We're not going to make it another fifty miles."

It was the middle of the night, the kids were sleepy, and the parking lot was deserted. The moon cast shadows from the unlit gas pumps and the log building that served as the office and store was dark. Ken's little band piled out of the truck to stretch and take a look around.

Ken leaned against the truck and smoked a cigarette, counting off his options. There was a phone booth at the edge of the parking lot, but who would he call? One of them could hitchhike to Helena, but that would be tough in the middle of the night. Or they could all just go to sleep until the station opened in the morning. Five people in the cab of a truck. Or on the gravel parking lot. In the cold with no blankets. Ken threw down his smoke and ground it out.

Just as Ken was shaking his head to himself, wondering what he'd gotten himself into, Eddie Number Two came around the corner of the station carrying a five-gallon can of gas.

"Look at this," he said, holding out a rolled up piece of paper. "It was stuffed under the handle."

Ken read it. "If you need this take it, but leave me the money to pay for it."

They looked at each other and laughed. "See, Man?" said Eddie. "These things happen."

Ken poured the gas in the tank, put his own ten dollar bill under the can's handle and put it back behind the station. Then they piled back in and headed for MacDonald Pass.

By the time they rolled into Helena, Ken wouldn't have been surprised if they pulled into a village of teepees with smoke curling out of the smoke holes. What happened was that they found a phone booth in a little shopping mall, and Eddie Number One went to make another call. It had been a long night, and Ken was feeling a little disoriented. His twenty-mile tow had turned into one hundred fifty, into country he'd never seen before. He seemed to have crossed over into another culture, and he really didn't know what to expect. He'd come to feel he had a stake in getting his clients safely home, but there was an edge of unreality to the whole trip. Then Eddie Number One came back from his call.

"We've got to meet someone here, Man," he said.

Ken thought – now what? His faith wavered, and he envisioned a drug deal going down around the corner. Maybe Eddie would hand him a stack of bills from a bank job, with a dye packet ready to explode. He looked around and said, "I need to get going pretty soon." Time wasn't really the issue, but he couldn't put his unease into words.

"Don't worry," said Eddie. "It won't take long."

They waited. The kids were asleep, and the adults leaned against the wrecker or looked in the shop windows at western clothes and chain saws.

"In Portland, I wouldn't stand around like this at night," Ken told Eddie.

"You from Portland?"

"Just moved here. Not even a year ago."

Eddie looked away from Ken, over toward where the sky was starting to get pale in the east. "You'll do OK here," he said.

After a while a little white Toyota Corolla rolled into the lot. The driver shut off the engine, but didn't open the door. Ken was ready for anything as he watched Eddie walk toward the car and open the door. He put himself between Ken and the driver, and Ken's anxiety level went up as he wondered what they were hiding.

Then a little Indian woman got out, in a long dress and long braids. Eddie bent down to give her a hug.

It was Eddie's mom. She walked over to Ken and took his hand.

"Thank you for bringing my boys home," she said. She patted his arm, and then reached into a backpack. "I'm so sorry to be late. I had to find an ATM that would take my card." She pulled out $150 in twenties and tens and gave it to Ken, and he couldn't help himself. He bent over and gave her a hug.

All five Native Americans got into the two-door Corolla, which didn't seem much bigger than the cab of the tow truck, and Ken decided not to ask for the gas money. This made a much better ending; the little car riding low on its suspension, the fine little woman driving off with her car full of wandering boys.

But then the brake lights came on and Eddie Number One got out and opened the trunk. It was packed to the top with cigarettes, and he handed Ken four cartons of Marlboros. Then he grabbed one for himself.

"Later, Man," he said to Ken, and touched the carton to his forehead in a salute. "It was a good night."

Chapter Seven • The Worst Things to Find in a Car

If you tow abandoned cars, or store them, or know someone who does, you understand that these vehicles are often home to remarkable collections of stuff. They can be the poignant landmarks of a life caught by outrageous fortune, or the junk left behind by someone who walked away from a bad deal. Either way, beyond certain obligations to the state and the previous owner, you are free to use these items to upgrade your cookware, improve your tool library or get a good start on back-to-school clothes for the kids.

But sometimes you might wish you'd minded your own business. Ken had a friend called Billy Rock Star who owned a big salvage yard full of wrecked imports. Billy favored Bruce Springsteen, and The Boss' music blasted from the speakers throughout the yard. One day Billy went through a wrecked Honda that had just been towed to the yard, with a back seat piled high with formal clothes, champagne bottles and glasses, and rock-hard wedding cake. On the floor of the back seat, under a layer of crumpled wrapping paper, Billy found a woman's high heeled shoe. With a foot in it.

Ken's towing colleagues have found bowling balls, pool cues, Dear John letters, handcuffs, eviction notices, report cards, and once an envelope filled with letters to a parole board. One of Ken's personal worst was a photo album full of old family pictures. The highway patrol called him to the tow the abandoned car, and he learned from the officer that the owner had been on his way home from his brother's funeral.

But the very worst thing that Ken ever encountered was not in an abandoned car, but in the cab of his own wrecker. It was a spectacularly hot August day, when just opening a car door meant risking burns. Heat waves rose from the roof of the Ford van that was blocking exit 75 when Ken arrived. Five more cars were backed up behind it, impatient to get off Interstate 90.

Ken pulled onto the gravel shoulder and did a quick assessment. The driver must have tried to turn around after he had trouble, because the van was sideways on the pavement, and close enough to where the road narrowed at the cattle guard that no one could drive past. The first thing to do was clear the exit, and Ken positioned his truck to hook up the front of the van. As he was maneuvering, he noticed that the two people in the van nearly filled the visible space behind the windshield. He hopped out to talk to them.

Before he reached his own back bumper he heard the shouted words bouncing around inside the van and tumbling out the window. "Idiot" was high on the list, along with "If you hadn't…. "If you only…." and "You always…" All that stopped as Ken reached their driver's window, when the man and woman turned to him and smiled. They were huge. Their broad, puffy faces were cartoonish in their sudden, bland friendliness. The man pushed his balloon arm out the window and offered his hand.

"Rupert Clouse," he said. "Listen, all you gotta do is just get under there and get that fuel pump and just slap another one in there and it'll be fine," he said. All his exposed skin was drenched in sweat, and his hand felt oily. His wife took one look at Ken and turned to look out her window, her limp ponytail brushing her bulging shoulders.

"OK, we'll get to that in a minute," said Ken. "Let's just get you out of the road first." He tried to let go of Rupert's hand, but the man kept hold.

"I'm all crippled up, you see," Rupert said. "I got the diabetes. I went and saw my doctor last week, and you know he said I have to be careful. Otherwise I'd do it myself. Just pull that fuel pump out, slap in a new one."

At this, Mrs. Clouse whipped back to face her husband. "Do it yourself?" she shouted. "Do it yourself? You idiot, you don't do nothin' yourself. Just shut up. Just shut up."

Rupert winced as the words pounded his back, but he spoke to his wife without turning. "Keep your trap shut, Betty," he said in a lowered voice, not losing his smile.

It was disconcerting for Ken to have Rupert speak with such venom, even though it was directed at Mrs. Clouse, and he took a step back. "I'm just going to get you hooked up now," he said, and went to work.

In ten minutes he had the hooks and chains on the van and was ready to hoist the front off the ground. He approached the driver's window again.

"You guys can ride with me in the wrecker," he said.

Rupert shook his head and adopted a mournful expression. "Can't do that," he said. "My legs are all stove up. I'd be out there with you if I could. My legs couldn't stand it."

Ken didn't push it, since he doubted the Clouses would fit in his truck anyway. He pulled the winch lever and the front of the van rose into the air. He watched it for balance, and it rocked gently with the movements of Rupert and Betty, who had returned to shouting and gesturing at each other. "Idiot!" "Jerk!" "Retard!"

Ken's shirt was stuck to his back when he climbed into his truck, and his steering wheel was nearly untouchable. This was starting to look like a call he shouldn't have taken, but there was no turning back now. He pulled out slowly, checking the van in the rear view, and headed for a shade tree he knew of, across the street from the Panther Express gas station and grocery, in Alberton. He could get something cold to drink there, and take a look at the van. Maybe it really was the fuel pump.

Ken drove the wrecker up the short hill that lead into town, mindful that he had people in his towed vehicle. Two boys on bikes cut in front of him at the top of the hill, their dogs running beside them. The Rottweilers made for the gravel shoulder, picking their feet up high off the hot pavement, and panting furiously. The boys turned and waved before they rode into Panther Express parking lot, and Ken drove under the tree and stopped. What he wanted most was to get this tow over with, but as he let the van down he could see no quick way out. He decided to try talking to Betty this time, and walked to her door.

"If you want to wait inside there," he gestured toward the little grocery, a white frame building with two gas pumps out front, rental movies and quarts of motor oil in the window. "It's cool inside, and you can get a pop or something."

Betty started to say something, opening her door as she spoke, and two balls of fur streaked out and ran into the street. They were Shih Tzu dogs, and Betty shook her head and glared at Ken.

"Now just look at that," she said. "We'll never get them back in." She started the process of getting out of her seat, alternately holding her breath and sighing. She swung one leg around and shifted her weight, and she reached her hand out to Ken for balance just as the Shih Tzus raced back around the front of the van and headed into the weed field south of the road. Close behind were the Rottweilers, and in a distant third were the two boys.

When Betty realized that the law of the jungle was about to rule against her dogs, her eyes blazed and an anguished cry rose from her mouth. "Aaaahhh!" she shrieked. "The dogs! The dogs! They're going to kill them!"

Ken watched the two big dogs chase the two little dogs through the field, thinking she might be right. It was like rabbits running from coyotes; the Shih Tzu's lightning-fast lane changes were working for now, but how long could they hold up? The boys were shouting, stumbling over clumps of knapweed and hidden ditches while their dogs ignored them. Betty was moaning beside him, bug-eyed and open-mouthed, wringing her hands.

Ken leaned against the van, then pushed away when it burned his back. There was no way he could charge enough to make this tow worthwhile, and he was ready to lift the van back up and tow the whole mess to Missoula, leaving the dogs to certain death, when they turned and headed his way. They whipped past Ken, dodged around Betty's legs and into the back seat of the van. The Rottweilers ground to a halt at her feet, looked up at her, and trotted off.

Ken looked at Betty, who was cooing at her dogs, and then at Rupert, who was crammed into his seat and staring, open-mouthed.

Rupert pulled himself together. "OK, then," he said. "Now, if you just get my scooter out of the back, you can get started on that fuel pump."

Ken stared at him. Scooter? He walked around and opened the back door. Sure enough, behind coolers and suitcases and cardboard boxes he could see an electric scooter as big as a golf cart. No way was he going to wrestle it out in that heat. Rupert and Betty had started bickering again, and Ken wondered if the highway patrol would drop him from their call list if he just unhooked the van and left.

Instead, he thought about the fuel pump. The engine in a 1985 Chevy van sits just about over the front axle.

You can check the oil and the radiator by opening the little hood in front, but to get to anything serious you have to remove what is called the doghouse. The doghouse is actually inside the van, between the front seats, and though it's upholstered and trimmed to look like part of the van's interior, when you take it off you're suddenly right there in the oily, greasy world of the internal combustion engine.

Rupert had found the strength to slide out of the van and make his way across the road to the Panther Express without his scooter, and he and Betty stood behind the window in air conditioned comfort, watching as Ken climbed into their van. He was aware of the Shih Tzus watching him from the back seat as he looked grimly at the spider web of wires running in and out to switches and tape decks and add-on lights and speakers. After fifteen minutes of following wires and disconnecting fittings, fixing a map of the wires in his head so he could put them all back, sweat dripping into his eyes, he popped the latches on the doghouse and lifted it from the engine. The carburetor, valve covers, and plug wires were all fuzzy with road dirt stuck to oil. In five minutes Ken knew that the fuel pump had nothing to do with the problem.

The Clouses were now headed back with cans of 7-Up. They kept a good distance between them as they walked, each with a rolling, wide-spaced gait. Ken could hear them muttering at each other, and the insults seemed to hover over their heads like words in cartoon balloons. The balloons popped when Ken spoke.

"If one of you could turn the key, I think I found what's going on," he said when they got close enough. He had pulled off a plug wire, and was holding the end close to bare metal, checking for spark.

"You look at that fuel pump?" Rupert asked.

"I don't think that's it," said Ken. "Just turn it over a few times and…"

But Betty was already at the driver's window, and she reached in and turned the key.

In the 1970s, General Motors started replacing the points in some of their distributors with what they called HEI. It stands for high energy ignition, and it delivers up to 50,000 volts to the spark plugs—twice what the older ignitions put out. When Betty turned the key, all those volts shot through the system, arched toward the metal, and shot instead into Ken's fingers, which had edged into that critical space. It slammed him backward, which in this case was up, and his head hit the rear view mirror like a ball into a bat.

Ken climbed out of the van. Blood trickled onto his temple as he backed away, rubbing his hands on his coveralls. The Shih Tzus revved up into a delirious bout of barking and jumping at the window, clawing madly at the side window glass. Betty glared at Ken.

"Shut that door," she demanded.

Ken stared at her. He was stunned from the electric shock, but he knew when to cut his losses. He wiped the blood on his sleeve, leaned back in and set the doghouse cover on the engine amid the doggy cacophony. "You guys are going to have to sit in the wrecker with me," he said. "I can't let you ride in the van all the way to Missoula." A creepy sense of foreboding was settling over him, but the only thing to do was keep moving.

Rupert and Betty did fit in the cab of the wrecker. Betty got the window seat, with Rupert crammed into the middle, surprisingly silent about his fuel-pump theory. Ken leaned against his door, arm out the window. Thirty miles to Missoula, he thought, *I can do this*.

But before Ken even shifted out of first gear, Rupert straightened in his seat.

"Oh, oh," he said. "I have to use the bathroom."

Ken took his foot from the gas and they slowed. "Panther Express has a bathroom," he said.

"No, no, I can't go in there," said Rupert, shaking his head sadly. "I looked in there. It's not a clean place."

Ken knew it was just a normal gas station bathroom, but he didn't push it. "OK, well there's the Sidetrack," he said, nodding down the street toward the little café, a few blocks away.

"Oh, well, I don't know," said Rupert. He was fidgeting ominously, looking around as though an enemy were closing in. "I guess if you hurry."

Ken looked at Rupert. Hurry? The café was thirty seconds away, but Ken hit the gas anyway. He felt the weight of the van as they accelerated, saw the kids on their bikes again in the side mirror, and sensed the tension in the cab as Rupert squeezed up his face in worry. Then, suddenly, Rupert smiled.

"Oh, never mind," he said. "Too late."

Ken's heart sank. He took his foot from the gas again and the wrecker shuddered a little from the rocking of the van behind. "Too late?" he said.

Rupert grinned. "Yup," he said. "I just crapped my pants."

Betty looked at him, and her face transformed into a delighted grin like switching on a light. "No you didn't, Hon," she said. "Remember? You borrowed a pair of my underpants this morning when you couldn't find yours. You crapped in my pants!"

Rupert and Betty looked at each other and broke into blissful peals of laughter. The insults were gone, and they were like kids who had played a trick on the teacher. Rupert turned to Ken.

"I crapped in my wife's pants," he said, slapping Ken's leg. "Get it?"

Ken got it. The pungent evidence filled the cab like smoke, and Ken pushed his speed as far as he could through town, angling his hand to direct the air into his face. He felt as though he'd stepped into an alternate universe, one where none of his skills as mechanic, driver, or diplomat mattered, and where insults had shape and aromas had color. He started counting mile markers.

Out on the highway, the air improved with speed. The human brain mercifully blunts the perception of smells over time, and as they neared Missoula, Ken began to think that this tow call might someday end. He tried a little conversation.

"So, what are you guys doing over here in Montana? Vacation?"

Betty released another of her newfound laughs, and Rupert patted her leg before he answered. "Oh, no," he said. "We're moving here. We just love these wide open spaces. This is Big Sky Country." Rupert looked at Ken. "We came to homestead some land. We're gonna be your neighbors."

Chapter Eight • Wired

"I got a guy here, out of gas."

It sounded like a typical tow call. Ken's answering service called with the message about a guy who got a ride to the River Edge Motel, thirty miles west of Missoula. River Edge was a little hotel with a bar, restaurant and campground right on the Clark Fork River. It's also right on Interstate 90, so people with car trouble tended to end up there pretty regularly.

When Ken dialed the call-back number he got the bar. And something in the bartender's voice sounded like a warning.

"Where's his car?" Ken asked.

A pause. Then, "Can't really tell."

OK. Put him on."

Another pause. "That probably wouldn't be a good idea."

Ken hung up and stared out his window for a minute. The bartender obviously hadn't hit it off with the guy. But by that time Ken had been dealing with misfits in shaky situations for more than 20 years, and he had a high tolerance for weirdness. Just listening to difficult clients was often enough to win them over, and a few sympathetic nods could buy enough goodwill to get through an uncomfortable tow. Besides, some tough cases turn out to be smart, sociable people temporarily disabled by their automotive nightmares.

Ken put a full gas can on the back of the tow truck and headed for the River Edge.

When he saw the guy, the phone conversation made more sense. "He was sort of buggy-eyed. Tall and skinny, clothes all dirty and ragged," Ken told me. "I try not to judge people on how they look, but this guy was really squirrely."

His judgment was right on. Every sentence the guy said was slightly off the mark. And every time he spoke, he included the phrase, "long barrel."

"So, you're out of gas today," Ken asked, going for a friendly, casual tone.

"It's a '69, '73 Buick four-door, Ford truck with a big block, long barrel," the guy answered. He wiped his nose on his sleeve and nodded.

The guy looked over Ken's shoulder as he spoke, as though he were talking to someone else. Ken glanced behind him, then forged ahead.

"So, is it a Ford or a Buick?" he asked. Not that it mattered, but the guy seemed to think it was important.

"It's a blue white long barrel," was the answer.

Ken thought about it. "OK, let's go," he said. They climbed in the tow truck and got on the highway headed west.

The guy settled in and lit a cigarette. He was so thin and ragged, that from the corner of Ken's eye he looked like an old blanket draped over the seat. Except that he kept nodding to himself and muttering. After a few miles, Ken needed more information.

"So where is it?"

The guy didn't hesitate. "Mile marker 63, 42, 30, west," he said. "Long barrel."

"OK," said Ken. Then, after a moment he asked, "Are we going the right direction?"

The guy raised his hand and pointed out the windshield in front of Ken, toward the east bound lane that was visible in patches through the trees in the median. His hand found a spot and followed it, moving toward Ken as they drove west, and when he was pointing at Ken's head he raised his thumb like the hammer of a gun, and fired.

"Long barrel," he said.

Ken looked ahead and started planning his escape. He now wondered if the guy had a real gun somewhere, and if there even was a car. He cinched his seatbelt up tighter and watched the right-of-way for a good place to ditch the tow truck. The crazy guy would go through the windshield, but Ken might be able to walk away. Hands gripping the wheel, Ken made conversation.

"So where are you from?"

"Seattle, Olympia, long barrel." He pointed his gun hand and squinted at trees and rocks as he fired, the recoil bringing his hand toward his face.

The Fish Creek exit was coming up, leading to the overpass that would put them back on I-90 headed east. If there was a car there, Ken would put gas in it. If not, he'd figure out a way to dump his client and head home. But just a few miles after they crossed the overpass and headed east, there it was.

The old white LeSabre looked as though it had fallen off a truck hauling salvage to the crusher. The windows were gone, including the windshield. The quarter panels were rusted out, and full length of muffler and tail pipe had lost touch with the car except for where it joined the exhaust manifold in front. It swayed gently a foot below the back bumper. Ken pulled up behind the car and stopped.

"Buick, Ford. Long barrel," said Ken's passenger.

Ken said nothing.

Through the back window of the LeSabre Ken saw another man sit up. He looked back at them through the window opening, then slowly opened the door and got out. The guy had long white hair in a ponytail, and looked a lot like a spooky Leon Russell. He moved with a sort of dignity, but his eyes were flat. He stood on the road and stared at Ken.

By now, all Ken wanted to do was get away from these guys. "Let's do it," he said. He got his gas can from the back of the truck and poured it into the LeSabre's tank while the two watched. Ken turned to his client.

"Give it a try," he said.

The man folded himself into the driver's seat and turned the key. The starter cranked a few feeble turns, then wound down to nothing. Ken's client stared at him, and Ken stared back. The responsibility for getting them going had settled over him like a prison sentence, and there was no way out but to start the car.

He got his jumper box out and hooked it to the LeSabre's battery, and to give it a better chance he poured a little gas in the carburetor. Then he stepped over to where he could see his client inside the car, and nodded at him to try again.

With the turn of the key flames exploded from the carburetor with a boom that Ken felt as much as heard. He stepped back and looked from the engine to his clients. The Leon Russell look-alike was still serene, and Ken's client was smiling.

When the flames subsided Ken turned back to the engine. "I was thinking, 'What the hell?'" he told me. "Then I saw it. The throttle was wired completely open." The fuel line was dumping gas into the carburetor like a garden hose.

"What's this?" Ken asked them.

"Big block, short throw, long barrel," said the client from the driver's seat. He motioned toward his feet.

Ken looked inside the car, and saw that the gas pedal flopped uselessly on the grimy floor. It had obviously broken some time ago, and instead of fixing it these guys had just wired their throttle wide open. Who knew how long they'd been driving it that way. No wonder they were out of gas.

But the problem then was how to start this train wreck of a vehicle, and get it headed out of Mineral County. Ken had an idea.

"Those old automatics, you could get them going about thirty in neutral and drop it into drive. They'd start that way," Ken told me. "All I wanted was to get these guys as far away from me as I could, as fast as I could."

He got his wish.

"I got them back in the Buick and told them what to do. Then I lined up my big old push-bumper on them. And I thought, 'OK, boys, we're going for a ride.'"

The '64 LeSabre is a heavy car, but Ken pushed through his gears and stayed on the gas until he had them going about fifty. Kens' client and his friend kept their eyes on the road ahead as they accelerated, their hair rising in the wind. For a moment they looked almost peaceful, gliding along in their silent car.

Then Ken heard a big KABOOM, and a cloud of black smoke exploded out of the tailpipe. The old Buick shot ahead like the Starship Enterprise going into warp speed. It tore down the highway away from Ken as fast as its 40-year-old axles could turn, growing smaller until it disappeared around a bend in the road.

"The Leon Russell guy told me they'd meet me at the River Edge, give me thirty bucks," Ken told me. "But I knew it wouldn't happen. Once they got going, there was no way they could stop. And that was okay."

Chapter Nine • What's Good for General Motors

Ken tried hard to take every tow call that came his way. He felt the hard edge of the bottom line, but more than that he had a powerful, optimistic drive to succeed. He carried his pager with him everywhere, even when he was playing music seventy-five miles away in the Bitterroot Valley or up in Seeley Lake. Money from a gig was as important as money from a tow, and if he got paged while he was playing he'd hide from the bar noise and call back. He'd greet the client with a cheerful, "Hi, this is Ken at Nine Mile Towing. Did you call for a tow?"

"I got really skillful at putting things off," he says now. "I'd say, 'Gee, I'm really busy right now. Could we just pick that up in the morning?" And a lot of times, that worked.

But sometimes it had unintended consequences. After four or five years building his business, Ken felt comfortable enough to let his friend Bruce talk him into a day of golf instead of towing. It was Bruce's birthday, an afternoon so clear you could see from the Bitterroots to the Nine Mile Divide, with a gentle breeze and a warm sun. The cheerful brightness of the day pushed nearly all of Ken's misgivings about skipping work into a tiny corner, and he and Bruce were having a big time with their own good natured parody of wealthy golfers, putting and driving on the King Ranch course in Frenchtown. This would have been a good time to tell his answering service he wasn't working, since they were drinking margaritas, but when his beeper sounded he couldn't resist answering the page. A Chrysler van had limped into the River Edge Motel, and the owner wanted a tow. Ken got the number from his service and punched it into his cell.

Cradling his phone against his shoulder, he lined up a putt as he spoke. "This is Ken at Nine Mile Towing," he said, tapping the ball toward the hole. "You called for a tow?"

The ball circled the cup and rolled two feet on the other side, and Ken covered his phone with his hand as Bruce whooped in derision. Ken had to turn his back to hear the voice on the other end.

"I need a tow to Missoula," the man said. "My van quit."

"What's it doing?" asked Ken, his mechanic's instincts swimming to the top.

"Oh, the engine's blown, for sure," said the man. "I had it down in low and I barely made it."

For a moment, Ken slipped out of the alternate reality he and Bruce had constructed for the day and pictured this guy in his van. Struggling up hills and coasting down the other side, wondering if he'd make it to a town, anxious about finding help. But it had been too long since the last time Ken had fun, and the draw of the sunny day and the bright green grass won out.

Bruce had taken his turn and quieted down, so Ken turned back and scrutinized his putt as he answered. "I don't think I could get there for at least an hour, hour and a half." He walked around the ball to get perspective, then sighted down his club. "I'm really busy right now."

Bruce licked his finger and held it in the air, checking the wind direction for Ken's putt.

"OK, listen," said Ken. He planted his feet and took a few practice strokes, still bracing the phone against his ear with his shoulder. "I'll try to wrap this up and get over there as soon as I can." He stepped up to the ball, took one more look toward the cup, and stroked. The ball rolled across the green like a steel bearing toward a magnet, and dropped into the cup with a satisfying plop. Ken threw both hands in the air in triumph and the phone fell into the grass. He could hear the man's thready voice as he reached for the phone.

"- Lee Iacocca?" Ken heard when he got the phone back to his ear.

"What's that?" he asked.

"Do you think it would help if I called Lee Iacocca?" the man said. He had a regional accent that Ken couldn't identify, and he sounded genuinely concerned.

Ken plucked the golf ball from the hole and climbed into the cart with Bruce, who was draining the last of his margarita. "Lee Iacocca?" Ken said, giving Bruce a look. "Sure, go ahead and call him. Couldn't hurt."

Four hours later they had finished eighteen holes and Bruce was wasted. Ken had quit drinking when he committed to the tow, but he was tired from the long day in the sun. Being with Bruce on his birthday was a good time, but it was exhausting. Ken dropped him off and went home for the tow truck and a sandwich, then headed for the River Edge Motel.

Driving the truck brought Ken back to real life. The familiar sound of the engine winding up as he climbed the on-ramp to Highway 90 focused him, by the time he pulled into the gravel lot at the old, one story motel on the edge of the Clark Fork River his blood alcohol content was near zero. Ken was barely out of the truck when the man came to the door and waved.

He was a tiny, dark-haired guy in polyester and gold chains, but with none of the swagger that implied. He held his hand out toward Ken like a host inviting him into a reception, and when Ken stepped into the room his first impression was that the bed, chairs and floor were covered with soccer balls. The balls turned out to be dogs – Boston terriers that leaped on and off the bed and rose up to paw frantically at Ken's pant legs, sneezing and snuffling and spinning in circles. Ken backed up to take it in.

"We were in Seattle," said the man, whose name was something like Louie. "At the dog show." He went to his suitcase on the dresser and pulled out two blue ribbons. "We won two firsts," he said.

Ken liked dogs, but this menagerie raised some questions. Would they ride in the van behind the tow truck? Did they have cages? Did they need to go out?

"They were all in the show?" he asked.

"Oh no, just Lottie and Blue Man. The rest came along for the ride."

Ken took a deep breath and let it out, thinking wistfully of the golf course. Then he said, "OK, let's get you hooked up." He turned and went out the door, with Louie behind him.

"I called Lee," he said. "He said he'd take care of it for me."

"That's good," said Ken. "That'll be a help."

The dogs did have cages, and they did ride in the van. Louie seemed a little uncomfortable in the clutter of the cab of Ken's truck, but he settled in and pretty soon he was smiling at the scenery and chatting about dog shows. But it had been a long day, and by the time they made it the thirty miles to Missoula, Ken was ready to finish up and go home.

They still had to go five more miles across town to Grizzly Motors, and rush hour traffic was bad. Ken was starting to worry that the service department might close. He shouldn't have wasted so much time on the golf course. He should have had his mind on business, on paying the bills.

And then there was the Lee Iacocca fantasy. Ken hoped believing he had pull with the former CEO of the Chrysler Corporation didn't mean the guy's insurance was bogus too.

They made the left turn into Grizzly Motors and pulled into the lot just as the service guys were leaving, all of them coming out the door and heading for the lot. Ken's heart fell. Now he would be stuck with Louie and the dogs until tomorrow. He'd have to drop the van and find a motel that would take ten dogs.

Ken sighed and shut off the truck. One of the guys was headed his way, probably to tell him where to put the van. He looked a little worried, probably anxious to get home. Ken rolled down his window.

"Is this the van from Alberton?" asked the service guy.

Ken hesitated. How did he know that? "Yeah," he said. "Where do you want it?"

The other service guys gathered around the wrecker and the van, watching Ken and Louie and glancing at the van, which sounded like a kennel.

"Right inside," said the guy, nodding to the bay door that was rising as they spoke. He looked across the cab at Louie. "We've got a new engine ready to go in, Sir. Get you going in just a few hours."

Then he turned to Ken and frowned. "Where've you been?" he said. "We've been waiting for this guy for hours, ever since we got the call from Detroit."

Ken looked at him. "Lee Iacocca?" he asked.

"The one and only."

Chapter Ten • A Real Man's Tow Truck

"It's got muscle you can depend on – you'll never wake up wondering why you got it."

"Quick Pick – designed for a large number of tows in a short period of time, ideal for impounding or repossession work."

"Midnight Express – capable of hooking up parallel-parked vehicles at up to a 90 degree angle"

"The Sliding Rotator – A real man's tow truck"

These are the trucks that warm drivers' souls. Gleaming proudly in full-page ads in The American Towman magazine, they are sleek and shiny, beautiful in their massive lines and understated power. They are far more than transportation. Even more than tools, they are the juice that defines the trade.

And Ken is, after all, a tow truck driver. Next to The Sliding Rotator, his 1980 Chevy was starting to seem a little shabby. It was on its third engine and transmission, and had almost 700 thousand miles on the rest. The heater stayed on until he pulled the wires for the summer, and if you lifted the floor mats you could see the road racing by underneath. Only a select group of close friends knew how to turn the key just right to start it.

So when he saw the 1989 Ford F-700 on eBay, he fired off an email. The bid was only $7,500, and it wasn't moving. Ken allowed himself to dream.

At that time, a brand new one-ton truck like Ken's Chevy would have cost about $60 thousand. You might have picked up a used one for anywhere between $10 thousand and $30 thousand, but that's just the start of the expenses. At that time, towing insurance in Montana was about $6 thousand a year. Every few years, tow trucks need six good new tires, for about $150 each back in the 1990s. Add up the loan payments, the gas and oil, the inevitable mishaps and malfunctions that must be fixed, and you'll come up with more than a thousand dollars a month in basic expenses.

Ken was spending about that, on a truck with a radio that didn't work, a broken windshield and no rear brakes. He missed out on the eBay Ford, but he struck up an email conversation with the seller. The guy had a big towing outfit in California, and he told Ken later that he grossed three million dollars the year before, mostly towing and impounding cars for the police. It turned out he was selling about 25 used trucks, and he had just the one for Ken. It was a great deal – the right engine, the right transmission, great price. They agreed on $9,000 for the truck, and Ken sent a $500 deposit and got ready to fly to San Diego. The only stipulation he made was that he wanted to drive it first.

Ken had his tickets and his bag packed when the seller called back.

"He told me they screwed up, sold the truck by mistake," said Ken. "But they had another one. It was an F600, a little smaller, but according to the guy it was really a better truck."

Telling me this story, Ken smiles at this part. It's such an obvious bait and switch, he can't believe he fell for it. But Ken remembers himself as the hopeful buyer, the Montana boy ready to pack some good clothes for a trip to the city. Clean jeans, nice shirt, American Towman belt buckle for a touch of irony, and his new wallet with a pile of hundred dollar bills.

"I didn't really want an F600, but he talked it up," said Ken. "Told me if I didn't like it, he'd give me my deposit back and pay for my trip." Ken had his ticket, he had his cowboy boots shined, and the momentum carried him forward. He got on the plane in Missoula, and flew out over the Bitterroots toward the coast.

As soon as Ken got to downtown San Diego, an ominous dread started to creep into his usually cheerful disposition. If this transaction were happening in

Missoula, or even big-city Billings, someone would have greeted him with a handshake and a clap on the back, a few stories about old trucks or old drivers, and advice on the best place for dinner and a beer. But in this city, people either looked away or glared at him with open hostility. Ken found his way to the shop, growing more uneasy with every step, and found a locked door next to a sliding glass window. A surly woman slid open the window and eyed Ken.

"Yeah, whataya want?" she demanded, her face slack with disdain.

"I'm here to see Steve," Ken answered, trying out his usually winning smile.

The woman stared at him. "Yeah, right," she said. "And who are you?"

"I'm Ken Field," he said, a little deflated. "He's expecting me."

The woman slammed the window shut, and Ken could hear her shouting to someone. Finally the door buzzed open, and he went in.

The place was huge. It seemed like a hundred people were working there, towing cars in and out, cranking trucks up and down on lifts, shouting at each other. The noise was overwhelming, with the traffic outside and horns honking at the bay doors and impact wrenches chattering. The comfortable garage smells of gasoline and engine coolant only made the scene seem more bizarre, as though he'd stepped into an episode of "The Twilight Zone" – at once familiar and surreal. No one paid any attention to Ken as he stood there, wondering what he'd gotten himself into.

But he still had his eyes on the prize, and finally he caught the attention of a mechanic in blue coveralls. The guy was impatient at first, but then he remembered the Ford.

"Oh yeah," he said. "It's right over here."

Ken was a little surprised. The truck was up on blocks, and the wheels were lying on the floor amid grease guns and wrenches. He thought, *They knew I was coming today. What's the deal?*

The mechanic explained without being asked. "We noticed one of the brake cylinders was leaking, so we're fixing it." He turned away and spoke to Ken over his shoulder. "So you won't have any trouble on your way home. Come back tomorrow around noon, and we'll take it for a ride."

Ken hoped things would look up the next day, but it turned out to be cold and pouring rain. He jockeyed the truck through the lot for the test drive, the mechanic beside him calling advice on close calls with parked cars, and inched toward the street. It was an onslaught of headlights, horns honking and rain water flying from tires, but the truck was big enough to bluff its way into traffic. Ken exhaled a cautious breath and checked his mirrors as they came up to the first light. He put in the clutch and touched the brake. It went to the floor.

They were going slowly enough that the emergency brake stopped them. The mechanic looked over at Ken's foot on the pedal. "Oh yeah," he said. "You know, sometimes you have to re-bleed them." He offered Ken a friendly what-are-you-gonna-do shrug, but Ken could see the guy was ready with a hard look if that didn't work. Ken let it go.

He decided his mission was to get back to the shop without killing anyone, so he pulled into the turning lane to go around the block. The windshield wipers were clattering and clacking together, smearing the glass with an oily sheen, and when he turned on the defroster it didn't work. He glanced over at the mechanic, who was looking out his side window.

"Defrosters are kind of important in Montana," Ken said.

The mechanic turned to Ken. "Yeah, I'll bet," he said.

The light turned, and Ken eased off the clutch. The truck bucked and heaved, and the mechanic looked back out his window. Ken got it smoothed out without comment, but it was another nail in the coffin.

"I was fairly unimpressed," Ken told me. The big city craziness, the dark gray day with unrelenting rain, and the grumpy, condescending mechanic had disoriented him. He missed Tenley and the worn familiarity of home, even his old truck. But he couldn't give up.

"We went to the parking lot to try out the towing accessories," Ken said. "Everything worked great. The cables ran in and out smoothly, the boom went up and down. That was a big plus. It still could have been a good deal."

As they drove back to the shop, Ken battled with himself. "The little kid in me was saying, 'Oh, just buy it. It'll be fine.' I had $8,500 in my brief case, and I really wanted to drive home in a tow truck."

Inside the shop was the same pandemonium as the day before, and the mechanic had to raise his voice to be heard.

"OK, we'll get those brakes adjusted and you can get out of here," he said as he walked around to get in the driver's seat. Ken stood out of the way, trying to keep an open mind as he watched the truck roll backwards into the stall. As it came to a stop over the lift, Ken's confidence slipped another notch. The mechanic climbed down and reached under the truck to adjust the lift ramps.

"Another little problem," said Ken. "No brake lights."

Now the mechanic was losing his patience. He got to his feet and glared at Ken, then swung under the back bumper. Sparks flew behind the lights as he twisted the wires together, and then opened the driver's door and stomped on the brake pedal. The lights came on.

"So now you got brake lights, OK?" He held Ken's eye for a long moment before he hit the control for the lift. The truck rose slowly, rainwater dripping onto the oily floor.

Okay, just a loose wire. Could happen to anyone, Ken thought. He wandered around the truck, checking for rust or Bondo or anything that would jump out at him, but mostly dancing around the whole decision in his head. He really wanted a success story. Then he got to the open driver's door, where the seat was now at eye level. There was the fuse box, normally attached to the wall but now hanging loose. Inside, the colorful wires were tangled and patched together with wire nuts, and the bottom of the box was a drip of melted plastic.

"Shit," he thought.

"Ken Field," said a voice behind him. It was Steve, the owner. Finally.

Ken turned to see a guy who could have been selling aluminum siding. If he'd ever worked on an engine he'd quit long ago and gone for the winning smile and hearty handshake instead. He offered both to Ken, then nodded to the Ford.

"So what do you think? Did I tell you right?"

Ken could see he probably wouldn't get a sympathetic ear, but he gave it a shot. "I don't know Steve," he said. There's a few things wrong with it."

Steve's smile flattened a little. "Like what?" he asked.

Ken ran through it: brakes, wipers, defroster, lights, fuse box. "And you told me it was a four-speed," he said. "The last thing I want is a five-speed turbo."

Steve's body language had changed. His shoulders were forward, and he tipped his head forward. "It's a used truck, Ken. What do you want for $9,000?"

Ken gave it a beat, then said, "Well, I'd like to make it home."

It was a standoff, but Ken felt he had the advantage. Steve had offered to pay his way home, after all, if he didn't like the truck. "I'll tell you what," Ken said. "I'll come back tomorrow and take it out for twenty-four hours. I'll give you the money now, and you give me the title, but we'll write up an agreement that I get my money back if I don't want it."

Steve hesitated, and Ken could see that there was something else going on.

"I'd like to do that, Ken," said Steve. "I really would. But I've got a problem. I can't find the title."

Back in Montana, Ken still keeps his eye open for a good deal. A Steel Rustler might come up on eBay sometime. Or a Midnight Express might appear in the Missoulian newspaper classifieds, under the heading, "You'll never wake up in the morning wondering why you got it."

Chapter Eleven • Operator Out of Service

The Fourth of July can be a big day for towing. Lots of traffic, lots of overheated engines, lots of distracted drivers who lean over to pull a Coke from the cooler and wind up in the ditch. But one year Ken didn't do any towing on the Fourth. He put his pager in a drawer and headed toward Virginia City for a gig instead.

Virginia City is a town that started before Montana was a state, when there were still unfenced buffalo on the prairie and General George Custer was still alive. The mountains there, just north of Yellowstone Park, are mostly brown with fingers of green pine forest climbing their north slopes. The little streams are full of trout and dammed here and there by beaver. But something about these streams is odd – the ground beside them is too high in places and the bottom too deep, and they are lined with mounds of gravel that look like someone drove a Cat down the stream bed.

What really happened was that miners dug up the streambeds in the 1860s, looking for gold. Ten thousand people showed up after the Alder Gulch strike produced $30 million in gold, built a couple towns and then tore them down to look for more gold underneath. The strike also produced the Montana Vigilance Committee, a rowdy bunch of good old boys who decided they'd be the judges of who committed what crimes, and who ought to die for them. In the winter of 1864 they lynched twenty-two men, one of them a sheriff.

The folks in Madison County are mostly ranchers and loggers now, but a lot of the economy is wrapped up in summer tourists. Ken and his friend Ronnie, the bass player, packed up Ken's VW bus and headed for a weekend of playing music for some of those tourists. Ken's friend Earl had set up the gig, and had come up with the band name – the Oakie Drifters.

The VW was a good band van. Good on gas, and plenty of room for the bass, Ken's drums, and a few guitars just in case. Ken was happy to be driving somewhere that didn't involve setting out warning markers. He had packed a pair of shorts along with the jeans and cowboy shirts that are required apparel for rockabilly bands. They cruised past Missoula and Deer Lodge, crossed the Continental Divide at the top of Homestake Pass and then cut south at Whitehall.

But as they climbed the first hill, the grinding sound that Ken had been ignoring since Butte demanded to be heard. He had a good idea what it was, and he knew there was no way he could fix it in Virginia City. He only hoped they'd make it that far.

The first VW engines were air cooled. That is, they were encased in a metal shroud where a fan blasted them with air to keep them from overheating. In the early 1980s Volkswagen started putting water-cooled engines in their buses, which meant adding things like a radiator and water pump. Ken's bus was one of the first with this new technology, and that's where his trouble began. The water pump was making a noise like marbles in a can.

They stopped at the top of a hill and opened the little rear engine lid. With the engine running, Ken could see the pump wobbling around on its shaft – the bearings were shot. He stood up and walked over to Ronnie, who was having a smoke and looking down into the valley.

"Good thing it's mostly downhill from here," Ken said.

"It's that bad?"

"We'll get there," said Ken. "But we won't get back."

Ronnie looked at the van, packed full of instruments. Then he nodded down the road toward Virginia City. "What about Earl?" he asked.

"He'll have tools. But he won't have a water pump for an 84 VW."

There was nothing to do but head down the road, so they did. You could shut off the engine in an old VW without worrying about your steering wheel locking or your brakes turning flat and useless. So they coasted when they could, listening to the wind and tire noise as ranchers in old pickups passed them, eyes straight ahead. Once in a while a teenager in a shiny Honda would zip past, or someone in a seventies Chrysler with different colored fenders. Not much different from Nine Mile, but something about the country was starting to spook Ken. If you drive up in your tow truck to rescue people with flat tires or cooked engines, they don't care if your hair is in a ponytail, like Ken's. But it's a different story when you're in an old VW van full of guitars. And then there was the whole vigilante thing, a murky paradigm that has never quite disappeared from the Montana consciousness. It took a hundred years for anyone to even question whether those guys might have been pushing the line a little. Ken looked at the trees alongside the road, and wondered if any were old enough to have held a hangman's noose.

On the straight stretches, Ken started the engine and drove, shutting it off again for the descents. They passed little crossroad towns with names like Parsons Bridge and Silver Star, pretty much following the Jefferson River to Twin Bridges, then taking highway 287 to the southeast, along the Ruby River. Ken was starting to worry about getting to the gig on time, but Ronny rode with his elbow out the window, as relaxed as if he were on vacation. He gazed at the scenery gliding past.

"There's gold in them thar hills," he said.

Virginia City has wooden sidewalks, false-front saloons and a Boot Hill cemetery. It has gift shops and restaurants and a playhouse, and every summer day it's packed with tourists. Ken and Ronnie rolled into town with the rattle in the back so loud people on the sidewalk were turning to look. Ronnie gave them little nods and waves.

Ken knew there was a cold beer with his name on it at Earl's house, but first he had something important to do. Call Tenley.

"Nine Mile Towing," she said into the phone.

"Hi, Hon."

"Hey, what's happening? Did you get there?"

"Well yeah."

"Yeah, but what?"

"I need you to drive the tow truck over here. Tomorrow."

Silence. Then, "OK."

Ken hung up and smiled. *Tenley to the rescue*, he thought.

Chapter Twelve • A Long and Winding Road

The next morning Tenley put a change of clothes into a bag and pulled on some old jeans and her cowboy boots. She put her hair in braids to keep it in line, and set her guitar in the passenger seat of the truck. Then she stood in her doorway and took a last look around. Her cowboy hat lay on top of the stereo. The hat spoke to her. It said that the trip would be more than just a grinding drive over and another one back. It said *Take me with you. We'll have fun.*

She was used to driving her Subaru, so the tow truck felt huge and cumbersome at first. But once she got out on the highway and shifted into fourth, the truck found its rhythm. And after Tenley settled in for the drive, she noticed other drivers staring at her. Truck drivers especially, who sat high enough to see her, gave her little salutes and smiles. Pretty soon Tenley was singing, "I Want to Be a Cowboy's Sweetheart," yodeling over the roar of her engine. She put on her hat.

She saw her first breakdown somewhere between Missoula and Deer Lodge. A little Toyota pickup, pulled off on the shoulder with the hood up. She switched to the passing lane to give them plenty of room, and waved as she passed. The woman in the driver's seat looked stunned, and Tenley could see her in the rear view, getting out and standing with hands on hips, watching the tow truck motoring on down the road.

Then Tenley got it. They thought she was *their* tow truck.

The next disabled car was a newer Buick, and the guy saw her coming. He was standing behind his car by the time she got there, and had his hands in the air in a "what gives?" gesture as she sped by. Tenley smiled at him and shrugged, keeping her foot heavy on the gas. This was getting embarrassing. Even if she did stop, she couldn't help them. She'd towed cars before, but never without Ken to deal with all the idiosyncrasies of the old Chevy. No way was she going to hook up some guy's new Buick, him impatient, waiting for her to screw up. And the real tow truck was certainly on the way.

But that didn't help when the people stared at her helplessly, the heat shimmering off the pavement at their feet. The next breakdown was a farm truck, which hurt her to the core. She told herself if it was a woman driving, or if there were kids in the cab, she would stop. Even if it was just to wait with them until their own tow truck got there. But it was two guys, and one was talking on a cell phone. Tenley pulled her cowboy hat down low and kept her eyes straight ahead.

Meanwhile back in Virginia City, the Oaky Drifters were recovering from the night before. You don't play until 2:00 in a bar with a hundred tourists and locals pushing and shoving on the plank floor and wandering in and out through the Gunsmoke swinging doors, and survive unscathed. Ronny and Earl were having red beers, and Ken was thinking about Tenley.

Calling her had seemed like the answer the night before, but now he was worried. The tow truck had a lot of miles on it and though the current engine was holding up, it wasn't perfect. Everything in the truck required some kind of trick to operate. Tenley knew not to turn the key all the way to Accessories – if you did you'd have to take the switch apart to start it again. But that was easy to forget. And sometimes you just couldn't get it into gear unless you feathered the RPMs just right and shifted at the magic moment. Ken drank coffee and pictured Tenley on the highway. He hoped she was over the pass by now. But what if she had trouble? He felt like a doctor who gets sick and winds up in his own emergency room, looking up at nurses who treat him like a stranger.

Ronnie and Earl started loading the van to head to Norris, the tiny town about 30 miles away where Tenley was to meet them. Earl had set up a jam session there with some local musicians. Ken packed up his drums and climbed behind the wheel, thinking he was glad Norris was on the way home.

The best he could hope for was the drive-and-coast system he'd used the day before, but now it would be mostly up hill. He took a deep breath and started the engine, and it sounded even worse than he remembered. Ronnie looked at him from the passenger seat.

"Wind 'em up, head 'em out," he said. "Rawhide."

There was a good crowd of locals at the bar in Norris. They ended up with an electric bass and a pedal steel and a few more guitars, and they had a good time with some old Rock and Roll as well as some bluesy tunes. But in the back of his mind, Ken was watching Tenley drive the tow truck.

First he saw the setting sun shooting through the window and backlighting her hair into a golden halo. She had on a white cowboy shirt with pearl snaps, silver earrings, and that sparkly look she got when she was ready to go on stage. She was driving with one hand, her shoulders back, the wind in her hair.

But then worry took over, and Ken's vision switched to Tenley standing beside the truck on the roadside. Heat waves rose from the pavement, and steam hissed from the radiator. She had the hood up, and she was shaking her head as an old pickup rattled to a stop behind her. Two wiry old guys got out, and one was wearing a tee shirt that said, "Montana Vigilantes – Judge, Jury, Executioners." Tenley turned and sized them up, planting her hands on her hips, and Ken crashed his drumstick into his cymbal. What was that in the back of that pickup? A coiled up rope?

It was time for a break, and everyone went outside for air. They stood in the shade of the bar and lit cigarettes, and Ken kicked gravel around. Just as it was time to go back in, he heard a familiar sound.

Someone said, "Would you look at that," and he did. The old white tow truck rolled into the lot in a cloud of dust.

Tenley swung down from the cab carrying her guitar and grinning. She had on a tee shirt and jeans and she put on her cowboy hat as she walked toward them. Ken draped his arm around her shoulders and walked her into the cool bar, and the Vigilantes faded back into history.

"How was the trip?" he asked. "Any problems?"

Tenley ordered a beer and spun around on the bar stool to check out the room. "Oh, no problems," she said. "I had to go incognito a couple times, though. I was glad I wore this hat."

Ken frowned and started to ask what she meant. But the music was starting and Tenley slid off the stool, opened her guitar case and took out her Martin. Ken got his bass and stood it up, running his fingers down the strings. It would be a good story, he knew. They would add it to their archive of adventures and pull it out later, to laugh about it with friends. They had all the time in the world.

Chapter Thirteen • Locked out

"Nine Mile Towing, this is Ken."

"Hi. I locked myself out of my car."

"OK, who's this?"

"What?"

"What's your name?"

"Oh. It's Tina."

"OK Tina, where are you?"

"I'm in the kitchen."

Silence. Then, "Where's your house, Tina"

"Oh. It's in Arlee, Montana."

"Good. And where is it in Arlee?"

"Next to my Mom's"

Lockouts can be a good supplement to a tow truck driver's income. Most insurance companies pay about $25 a call, with extra for going farther than five miles or so. It's usually enough. But not always.

One January evening, in weather so cold the snow squeaked under foot, Ken took a call when he really shouldn't have. He only had about an hour to get to a gig in Missoula, and he'd be dressed in his musician clothes —clean jeans, snappy shirt, and cowboy boots with slippery soles. His drums would be in the van, and he didn't want them to get cold. But his answering service said the lockout was in Frenchtown, which is on the way, so he decided he could make the small detour, open the door, and get back on the road in plenty of time.

When he pulled into the lot at Frenchie's, it was clear who his client was. The little pickup was at the pump, and the woman was bouncing on her feet next to her driver's window. She was frantic.

When Ken walked over to the pickup, he saw why. Inside was a little black and white dog, maybe a Jack Russell terrier, jumping up and down and blowing snot on the windows. The engine was running, the heater was on full, and the dog was bug-eyed and panting.

And it was twenty below zero outside. "Why don't you wait inside?" Ken asked the woman. Not only was her nose red with cold, but she radiated a panicky tension that was already making him nervous. She barely heard him.

"I left the heater on," she cried. She could have said there was a bomb set to go off, by the dread in her voice. She put her hands on the glass like a mother

107

saying goodbye to her death-row son. "Pugsy, it's OK. It's OK. Mommy's here," she said. Pugsy snuffled at the glass, then bounced to the other window. Mommy followed.

"He does look warm," said Ken. He could have said, "This dog is toast," for all the attention she paid him. She was so focused on her dog that external events didn't exist for her. Ken could see what happened. Pugsy had watched Mommy go inside to pay for the gas, and then pawed at the windows until he hit the automatic door lock.

Ken went to the driver's window and tapped a wedge between the door and the door post to get some room to work. For years Ken used a collection of specialized tools to reach inside the door and trip whatever mechanism controlled the lock. He has an expensive set of tools that came with diagrams of the insides of all the different doors, and directions on how to use them. It was complicated and frustrating, and sometimes resulted in a disaster inside the door – electric windows that no longer worked and a door that was still locked.

Now he uses the Big Easy. It's an angled rod that fits through the space he opens with the wedge, and then opens the door by touching the electric door lock button inside the car. It can tap either the side you're working on or the opposite door. But this night, with Pugsy leaping frantically across the seat, it wasn't working. Every time Ken got the Big Easy lined up, Pugsy jumped on it. Then he would jump at the window, aiming at Ken's hand through the glass. Ken couldn't help jumping back. Pugsy's teeth clicked on the window, and Ken could see the dog's pink tongue behind the fog from his breath.

"Oh, god," moaned the woman. "He's going to hurt himself." She trotted back to the driver's side, her own breath clouding around her head as she pushed her face close to the window.

"See if you can keep him over here," said Ken, as much to keep Mommy away as the dog. He took out his wedge and went to work on the other side. But as soon as he started Pugsy was back at his window, tearing at the sill with his claws like a badger. Ken blew out a long breath. His own nose was running now, and his fingers were stiff and cold even through his gloves. He tried to focus on lining up on the lock button, but it wasn't working.

"I just didn't want him to get cold," wailed the woman. She tapped her window to call Pugsy back, and he leaped from side to side between them.

Other gas customers were beginning to stare, and Ken needed to get going to his gig. This job was shaping up as a battle between him and Pugsy, and Ken was starting to think the dog had the edge. He took off his gloves and shoved his hands into his armpits to warm them up before giving it another try. He didn't realize the woman had gone until he saw her trotting back from the edge of the lot.

She was carrying a rock the size of a Big Mac, hefting it like a weapon. As she got closer Ken saw that her face was set in a desperate frown. She was lifting the rock, getting ready to smash the window.

"Wait," said Ken, moving in to block her. He lifted the rock from her hand. "You don't want to do that. Side windows cost more than windshields," he told her, hoping to ground her with practical information. But she didn't even look at him. She put her mittened hands to her face in an agony of frustration. "I don't care," she moaned. "Look at him. He's dying."

Ken didn't think so. But he was considering the rock himself as he looked inside the cab one more time, wishing Pugsy would get his collar caught on the gearshift for just one minute. What he saw instead was the back window of the pickup.

How could he have missed it? The sliding windows in these pickups latched with a flimsy plastic hook. He dropped the rock and put his gloves back on. Then he grabbed screwdriver from his kit and climbed inside the little camper shell, and popped open the window latch. Hot, doggie air whooshed out into his face, but he managed to lean in and unlock the driver's door. He backed into the camper shell in time to avoid the tearful reunion between Pugsy and his mommy.

Just a week later Ken got another lockout call for the same location. It sounded ominously similar – a woman's car still running at the pump, locked with the keys in the ignition. Ken got there in half an hour.

The woman was at her car, but that's where the similarity ended. She smiled happily when she saw Ken, and laughed at her predicament.

"I can't believe I did this," she said. "I left the engine running so Buddy wouldn't get cold – then I just pushed the lock and shut the door."

There was no dog at any of the windows, and Ken was lost for a minute. Then he looked in the back seat – there was a baby in a car seat.

"Your baby is in there?" he asked, a little surprised. There had been nothing in the call that indicated he should hurry.

The woman laughed and looked in the window at her child. She smiled at the bundle of blankets with two chubby legs sticking out. "Yeah," she said. "But he's asleep. He doesn't have a clue."

Chapter Fourteen • If you tow it, they will come

It's a summer Saturday, and Tenley has the house to herself. Ken has just left for an out-of-town gig until the next day, and the kids are all somewhere else. She puts on a John Prine CD and turns it up. She puts on her swimming suit and pulls a cold beer from the fridge. In the back yard, shaded by Ponderosa pines, is an aluminum stock tank filled with cool water that reaches just above the seat of a low beach chair Tenley has placed inside. She smiles.

It had been a hectic week. Tenley worked for her friend Bruce every day, clearing brush around his new house, stacking firewood, hauling building scraps to the dump. And just existing next to Ken's life of tow calls and gigs was like walking head first into a gale. So now she welcomed the peace and tranquility that settled over her as she eased into the water. She leaned back in the beach chair and opened *The Perfect Storm*. John Prine and Iris DeMent were singing a tune about love in the midst of adversity. Tenley took a swallow of beer and closed her eyes.

"Hellooo?" came a voice from over the fence. "Anybody there?"

Tenley didn't move. Maybe she could just keep quiet and whoever it was would go away.

"Hellooo?" came the voice again.

Tenley had no doubt what was going on. It would surely be one of the typical bewildered travelers who wandered in from the highway on summer weekends, in need of gas or a tire or water for their radiator. Usually she was happy to help, but not today.

And this guy wasn't giving up. Maybe she could deal with it quickly and get rid of him. "Come on back," she called, and he did.

Telling the story later, Tenley shakes her head. "Of course he had to be this handsome biker dude, all decked out in leathers and a bandana. And there I was in my swimming suit, without even a towel."

All he needed was to use the phone. But that meant Tenley had to climb out of the pool and walk inside, with him behind her. With John and Iris singing a line about a girl getting it on like the Easter bunny. Tenley showed him the phone and went to grab a towel.

He turned out to be nice enough, no tics or fresh wounds. Tenley chatted with him about his Harley and the frustration of breaking down far from home. His girlfriend was waiting with the bike, in the shade under the I-90 overpass just a few hundred yards up the road. Tenley tightened her towel and wished him luck.

Then she got back in the pool and thought about life near exit 82. You couldn't see the Interstate from there, you couldn't even hear it. From where she sat, her view to the south was the red rock cliffs on the other side of the Clark Fork River, and the trees in between. But although the highway to the north was out of sight it still nagged at you, like a bad singer in a good band. Maybe she should write a song about needing to be close to something, yet yearning for distance. Her beer was still cold enough to drink, and she took a sip.

"Hellooo." This time it was a woman's voice.

"Shit," Tenley said to herself. Then she called, "Yeah?"

The handsome biker dude opened the gate and came into the yard with his girlfriend, a sturdy woman with tanned arms and freckles across her nose.

"Do you think you could sell us some beer?" she asked.

Tenley laughed. It was hopeless. She'd been dreaming to think she could have a quiet summer afternoon with a book.

At least this time she had a towel. She sold them a six-pack of Foster's and watched them walk back toward their motorcycle. Then she looked out the window at the

115

stock tank, her lawn chair, the book in the grass. The shadow of the pines had moved on, and the pool was baking in the sun.

It was a winter day when Tenley told me this story. But the frustration of losing that day of summer peace was still fresh. She put it like this:

"I said to myself, 'I'm not going to sit here and rescue people all weekend. Instead, I put the top down on the TR6 and took off for the Sportsman's Bar."

***

Tenley might not have given up on her peaceful day so easily if the biker hadn't been just one more in a long history of hard luck folks who showed up when Ken was gone. It seemed as though they waited around the corner until they saw him turn onto the on-ramp, and then knocked at the door.

It started soon after they moved in, when Tenley was operating the old store as a quick-stop grocery. Families on vacation drove in from the highway and bought snacks, and locals stopped in for milk or pop. One day a tall guy in cowboy boots walked in and closed the door. He looked at Tenley and said, "I don't want to hurt anybody."

Tenley gave that a moment. Then she said, "OK, what can I do for you?"

"I don't have any money," said the guy. He was tall and broad, and wore a bandana on his head. "But I need some beer."

Tenley looked at him. He wore a red and black plaid wool jacket with ripped elbows, and black jeans. "Maybe we can work something out," she said, and took him outside to their woodpile. Two hours later the wood was split and stacked, and the guy was into his first Foster's. He hadn't said a word since his first demand.

Now he tucked two six-packs under his arm and turned to leave, open beer in hand. Then he turned back. "I'm walking to Alaska," he said, and left.

***

Another day, a guy slipped in the door like smoke, and stood for a moment looking around. His eyes jumped around the shelves, catching on Doritos and cigarettes, and sliding over Tenley as though she weren't there. She was a little spooked.

"How ya doing?" she asked. "Did you walk in?" There was no car out front.

"Hitchhiking," the man said. He carried a hard-shell briefcase, and he pulled it to his chest when he spoke.

117

Finally he brought a can of pop and some cigarettes to the counter, and Tenley rung them up. She was eager to get him out the door. He reminded her of Peter Lorre in *Arsenic and Old Lace*.

"Three dollars," she said.

The man set the briefcase on the counter and finally raised his eyes to meet hers. "I'm looking for some property to buy," he said, his voice flat but insistent. He made no move to pay.

Ken was in the shop just a few yards away, and Tenley wished he'd chose this moment to take a break and walk up for something to drink. But he didn't.

"Yeah?" she said. "Most everything is already bought up around here."

He looked out the window as if to check if she were telling the truth, then back at Tenley. After a moment he opened the briefcase. It was stacked full of twenties and fifties. He pulled out a twenty and handed it to Tenley, then put the change in this pocket.

Tenley walked outside after he left, to see if he really was hitchhiking. She watched him light a cigarette and look east, then west as he exhaled the smoke, his back to her. Then he carried his case full of cash up the eastbound onramp and didn't look back.

Ken remembers a guy who needed a water pump, but after that was fixed it turned out he needed additional parts that would take a couple days to get. He seemed like a decent guy, and Ken and Tenley let him sleep on their couch for two nights. They fed him meals and he helped out a little with firewood, but Tenley was getting a little tired of having him around by the third day. That night he went with them for a beer at Larry's Six Mile Bar, and his alternate personality emerged. He got loud and pushy, and when he draped his arm around Tenley and started smooching her neck, Ken had had enough. He stepped in and put a sharper definition on the boundaries of the mechanic-client relationship.

They picked the guy off the floor and went home. He slept in his cold car that night, and chose not to wait for his parts before he got back on the road the next morning.

Then there was the day the guy pulled up in the mint, 1967 Plymouth station wagon. It was Christmas time, and Tenley had converted the general store into The Christmas House, where she sold vintage decorations, antique toys and handmade gifts. When the

Plymouth pulled up, everyone in the store went out to look at it.

"It was showroom quality," says Ken. "A little road dirt, but perfect chrome, big old white walls. The guy was really proud."

It came out that the driver's father had just died and left him the car. "I'm headed to his funeral now," he said. "Chicago."

Ken said, "Too bad, man." He was walking around the car, checking out the perfect taillights, when he noticed the casket in the back.

"Yeah," said the man. "He was quite a guy. That's him in the back."

Chapter Fifteen • A library of cars

Ken and Tenley's home at Nine Mile was a collection of contradictions. The vintage general store stood in front of an ordinary double-wide. If you looked out over the grassy field to the east, bordered by pines, you couldn't tell that Interstate 90 was just over the hill, humming with 75-mile-an-hour traffic.

And then there were the cars. On one side of a tall fence was a lush, green back yard that Tenley landscaped with a border of raspberries, sage and phlox. Her vegetable garden overflowed with fat tomatoes and cucumbers surrounded by basil and lavender. She dug a fire pit where she and Ken, along with whoever dropped by, could sit in lawn chairs and have some wine, maybe see what tunes came around on the guitars.

On the other side of the fence were cars. The towing business attracts them, and the population of mostly non-running vehicles rose and fell. Ideally they were invisible behind their fence, but sometimes a few spilled over into view.

For Ken the cars were part of his business. For Tenley, they were a thorn in her side.

"It was definitely a sore point," Ken says now. "She didn't want to be surrounded by cars."

But while the totality of vehicles weighed Tenley down, individual cars were a different matter. She was a musician and a song writer with the heart of a poet. For her, cars had stories of their own.

Here's how she put it: "Cars can be part of your family. When you see the truck towing it away, it can break your heart."

Tenley talked about walking down the rows in a wrecking yard, imagining each vehicle's history. There would be a Chevy that someone drove to the prom and a Cadillac that another couple fought over in their divorce. Maybe that Fairlane was a getaway car. And the older the car, the higher the likelihood that a baby was conceived in its back seat. It's like a library of cars, Tenley said, where everyone has a story.

She played starring roles in several car stories of her own, most notably British sports cars. When she was about six, she decorated a white Triumph with a brush and a can of house paint. Years later another Triumph would make her all-time favorite list. It was a TR-6 that she owned for twenty years and counted on as her getaway car. Like the best novel, it could sweep her away from real life when she needed an escape.

For Ken, a certain Ford Expedition spoke volumes. It was headed east on Interstate 90, driven by a woman with her kids in the back, when an elk bounded into its path. The people were unhurt, but the elk died and the truck's front was smashed.

A number of processes kick in after a highway accident, and in this case Nine Mile Towing got it all started. The tow went smoothly and the wrecked Ford made it to Ken's place. But things ground to a halt when the Montana Highway Patrol tried to verify the vehicle's registration. The license plates were issued by an entity that didn't show up in their search: The Ojibwa Nation.

Certain native tribes issue their own license plates, but the information isn't always shared nationwide. Ken noticed the plates, and the eagle feather decal in the back window, and he liked what he saw. Sure, the hood was buckled and the core supports were shoved into the radiator. But the vehicle had a good feel to it. Ken and Tenley both had a soft spot for Native American culture, and he was happy to give the Expedition a home while it was in legal limbo.

That limbo dragged on. The Montana authorities found the vehicle's registered owner, who was the father of the driver. But the Expedition had only liability insurance and no one came to claim it or to give Ken any money. He towed it behind the tall fence and relegated it to the back of his mind.

Many months later, Ken took another look at the Expedition. It had a lot of miles but the damage looked a lot worse than it was. If the owner would sign over the title in return for the cost of the towing and storage, Ken would be happy to make it his own.

There's a legal pathway for tow truck operators to get title to abandoned vehicles, and Ken followed it. But during the designated waiting period Ken had second thoughts. It didn't feel right to take the Expedition without ever talking to the owner. And another thing: He had learned that the owner's name was Dennis Banks.

"I thought, Whoa! I wonder if it's *the* Dennis Banks," Ken says. "It did have Indian license plates."

Back in the 1960s, Dennis Banks co-founded the American Indian Movement, or AIM. He was part of the occupation of Alcatraz Island and the siege at Wounded Knee in South Dakota. Over the years he taught at universities, acted in movies, wrote books, campaigned for justice for Indian people and spent a short time in prison.

Ken really hoped he also owned a 2002 Ford Expedition.

While he was thinking all that over, a guy from Minnesota showed up at his door.

"He said Dennis Banks sent him to pick up his personal belongings from the SUV," Ken says. "I asked him if it was *the* Dennis Banks. He laughed and said, 'Yep, that's him.'

The emissary, whose name also was Ken, gathered up the kids' toys and other items from the vehicle. But what Dennis Banks wanted most was the eagle feather decal. He got out a razor blade and tried to scrape it off the glass.

Not surprisingly, that didn't work. The decal stayed with the Expedition, which stayed with Ken and Tenley. With a new hood and radiator, it's still on the road.

"It's terrible on gas, but it just goes and goes," he says. "It has the heart of a lion."

Chapter Sixteen • Favors for Neighbors

"Tell me about other stuff you've towed, anything that isn't a vehicle" I ask Ken.

It's a Sunday evening, and Ken and Tenley are cooking dinner while we have some wine. It's a familiar setting and Ken is used to my tape recorder by now. But tonight I'm looking for something different.

The three of us remember the life-sized chrome horse, a sculpture by a local artist made out of bumpers and door handles and other car parts from a local junk yard. The artist asked Ken to load it onto a truck for him, but they both thought it would be interesting to see what some real horses thought of it first. When Ken set it down in a nearby pasture, the mares and geldings thundered up snorting and kicking, and then ran away and came back, circling the sculpture for a half hour before they were convinced it wasn't a horse.

Ken tells about the eight-foot culvert he towed that became an airfoil at about 40 miles per hour, lifting the back of the tow truck with a weird, zooming noise. And the piano he moved for his friend Bruce. Tenley remembers playing it as they made the last turns on the dirt road before Bruce's house, thinking about Jack Nicholson in *Five Easy Pieces.*

Then there's the safe. The lovely antique had been in the owner's family for generations, but in a botched attempt by two "professional safe movers" it wound up sliding down an icy hill and taking out part of her deck. The neighbor called Ken to help.

"It was this beautiful old safe," Ken tells me. "It had really ornate trim and it was painted with a western scene. It weighed about two tons." When Ken saw the safe, it had come to rest on its side, in front of a house on a steep hill. Standing nearby was the owner, who is a lawyer, and the two professional safe movers. She was calm, and the safe movers were taking a stab at keeping their dignity.

The safe seemed OK but the scene was a mess. The safe had knocked out the supports for her deck and one end now sagged. Not only was the ground steep, but it was also icy. Ken backed the wrecker down the hill as far as he could while the professionals harnessed the safe. They got Ken's hook into the harness, and it looked good. The safe rose slowly into the air.

Everything was still going fine as Ken drove forward up the hill, maneuvered the truck to aim its rear, with the safe hanging from the boom, toward the doorway of the house. He started backing down the hill, but eventually he had to touch his brakes and the safe started to swing. The weight of the safe on the downhill end of the truck battled the weight of the rest of the truck, and the safe won. Ken's front wheels came off the ground, and the whole thing started to slide toward what was left of the deck.

"It wasn't the first time I'd had my front wheels off the ground," Ken says. "I knew I couldn't count on my brakes, so I slammed the transmission into first and popped the clutch." Here he grips an imaginary steering wheel and looks over his shoulder, as though the safe is hanging behind him now. "I'm skidding sideways and sliding downhill, and the safe is swinging. It just barely missed hitting the house."

Two hours later the safe was inside and the lawyer was still being a good sport. The professionals had their heads down, packing up to leave. They promised Ken some free replacement car keys from their lock shop if he ever needed them, and hit the road.

Chapter Seventeen • Hit the Road, Jack

Right from the start, questions stacked up about the guy with the flat tire on Lookout Pass. First, why didn't he just change it?

Then there was Ken's fee. The call came from Allstate, where the client had towing insurance. But his limit was $80, and at 160 miles round trip it wasn't really worth Ken's time to drive up there. Would Allstate, or maybe the client, go a few more bucks?

The question of how to get hold of the client to see if he would pay above his limit had an answer. You couldn't. He didn't have a cell phone. He'd gotten a ride to the next town, which was in Idaho, to make the call. Now he was back at his vehicle, but would he still be there when Ken arrived? Probably not.

"These kinds of calls usually resolve themselves," Ken told me. "I get there and they're gone. Somebody stops to help, and they get it handled."

But it was a good day for a drive. Though there was still snow on the peaks, the air was warm and clear. Tenley packed some snacks and Ken put his jack and a lug wrench in their Saab – no need to take the tow truck all those miles just to change a tire. They had another cup of coffee and finished up a few chores around the house – Ken still felt sure Allstate would call back to cancel and he didn't want to leave too soon. His cell phone would be out of range in a few miles.

But after an hour the tow was still on, so they headed out. Their dogs, Boomer and Boozer, settled into the back seat and Tenley took out her knitting. Her daughter Anna, now 24 and living in Georgia, was pregnant and Tenley was making her a baby blanket. The rows of blue stitches grew as they sailed up the highway toward Lookout Pass, where Montana meets Idaho.

They drove past the little towns that slipped quickly by, with just a dozen or so buildings visible from the road. Some had storefronts that looked just like those from a hundred years ago, when loggers walked through the doors in cork boots. The timbered hills revealed just a few clear-cut patches, above brown fields not yet greening up with alfalfa. They also passed a few dozen sites where Ken had rescued cars and drivers over the past 15 years – this bridge and that curve in the road, mile markers 55 and 62, in the median just east of the Fish Creek Bridge. They talked about what they would do with the rest of the day, since Ken was sure the flat tire guy would be long gone when they got there. Drive on over the pass and have lunch in Wallace? Go up to the Lookout Ski Area and look around?

But just a few miles short of the top, there was the new Toyota 4-Runner, pulled off onto the gravel shoulder, leaning onto its flat tire. It was the left rear, and the spare was already out of its rack under the rear of the SUV. The jack and lug wrench were arrayed nearby, as though waiting for a yard-sale customer to inspect them.

As they pulled in behind the 4-Runner, Tenley put away her knitting and hid the cookies and the bag of chips under the seat. "We should probably look more professional," she said.

"Right," said Ken. He zipped up his jacket and tucked some errant strands of hair behind his ear, and got out. The client was walking toward them, smiling.

He was a friendly professor kind of guy, with an earring and thinning hair. He looked to be fiftyish, dressed in corduroy pants and flannel vest. Ken thought he had the look pretty well down.

The professor spoke before he got to the Saab.

"Help's on the way," he said. "But thanks anyway."

"I'm the help," said Ken.

The professor looked at him, and then the Saab. Tenley smiled at him from the front seat and Boomer and Boozer were up and churning around in the back.

"You're the tow truck guy?" he asked.

"Yeah, didn't figure I'd need the truck for this," said Ken. He walked over and looked at the jack, which was so new it shone like a nickel. The question hung in the air between them until Ken had to ask it.

"So," he said, as kindly as he could. "You didn't change the tire because...?"

Frustration entered the professor's voice as he ran a hand over his forehead. "It doesn't work," he said. "Look." He picked up the jack handle, and it did look awkward. There seemed to be no way to attach it to the jack that made sense.

But Ken had been around new-age jacks before. "Do you have a manual?"

The irony of the tow truck guy asking the professor why he didn't read his manual was not lost. But it lasted only the second it took for the professor to go look for it. In that moment, the passenger appeared from her side of the Toyota. And Ken began to see the rest of the story.

She was a big girl, younger than the professor but no coed. She was dressed so correctly it was painful to see. She might have worn a tee shirt that said, "I can climb a mountain, choose a fine chardonnay and harvest a garden without getting dirty." She said it instead with a dusty rose hemp top and bay leaf heather shorts with a stainless steel water bottle latched to a belt loop. She didn't smile.

The professor showed up with the manual turned to the right page, and looked sheepish as Ken put the jack together and fit it under the axle. The white paper with the diagram was like an indictment lying there in the gravel.

The professor said, "Hmm. Guess I should have read the directions."

His manner held a little apology and a little humor. And he had done everything he knew how to do, getting out the spare and the tools. Ken decided he liked him.

The passenger, who might have been his wife or girlfriend but was certainly not his friend, made a shift in her posture that exuded scorn and contempt.

"She was standing there with her arms crossed," Ken told me. "They waited at least two hours for us to get there. And now we're standing around this flat tire that took me about five minutes to change. She looked at him and her body language said, 'You worm.'"

Ken glanced at Tenley, still in the Saab, to see if she was picking up on the couple's dynamic. She was. She smiled and shook her head.

"OK," said Ken, turning back to his clients. "Here's the deal."

The deal was that he wanted to get away from this job quickly. But there was still the matter of the mangled tire. Fitting it into the spare tire rack under the car would be tough, and in this case he thought it might even be a bad idea. He foresaw a rough road for the professor, and wanted to give him every break he could.

"Let's just put this tire in the back of your truck," Ken said. "If we put it in the rack, it's out of sight. Too easy to forget, then if you have another flat you're stuck."

His offer was met with silence. Finally, the passenger said, "But our stuff is back there."

Sure enough, the back of the Forerunner was stuffed with bags and suitcases. Ken took one look and was ready to call it a day, he'd done all he could. But the professor rallied.

"No, that's a good idea. Then we won't have to get back under there to take it out again," he said.

Pretty soon the flat was resting in the back, segregated from the higher class items by a layer of towels. Ken started to close the lid, but the passenger stopped him. She had picked up the shiny new lug wrench with a towel, and was holding it like a dead animal. She glared at him, then set it next to the flat tire.

Back in the Saab, ready to leave, Ken said to Tenley, "I'm going to give them a few minutes head start, give them some privacy. It's the least I can do."

Tenley had the chips back out. "What do you mean?" she asked.

"He's an all right guy," said Ken. "He tipped me twenty bucks. But it was really hush money."

Tenley laughed. "So you're not going to tell anyone?"

"No, it was more like he was thanking me for not treating him like an idiot. Or for not being rude to his girlfriend."

They waited five minutes after the 4-Runner left, then headed west again toward the next exit. Lookout Pass gets steep at the top, and they gained enough altitude in a few miles that patches of snow appeared at the side of the road. Soon the sky was gray and drizzly, and the road had a skim of slush. Then, just a few hundred yards short of a wide pull-off at the top, they saw the professor's 4-Runner pulled over on the shoulder again. He was lying on his side in the slush, under the back of the SUV. His passenger had resumed her angry schoolmarm pose.

Ken thought, *Shit, did something go wrong?* He pulled over and started to get out before he realized what was going on. She'd refused to go on until they got that dirty tire out of their Toyota. The professor was wrestling it into its rack.

He edged out from under the SUV and sat up, and Ken stepped out of the Saab. "Everything OK?" he asked.

The professor gave him a resigned smile, and flashed two thumbs up, putting the best face on the whole fiasco. Ken's heart went out to him, and he gave a little wave as he got back in the Saab.

The only thing to do was drive away.

Chapter Eighteen • Forgetting the words

Tenley played a lot of music in Montana, with her band the Hot Tamales, with Ken and other friends who could put together a band overnight for a wedding or graduation, and with folks down at the local tavern who showed up with their instruments to jam. Her singing always lit up the room.

She was a sure bet as a performer, and one night in 2011 she filled in with Ken's regular band, the Revelators, when their lead singer hurt his back and couldn't make the gig. Ken was excited—he and Tenley hadn't played a real gig together in years.

They warmed up and started in with Jambalaya, a song Tenley had sung at least a hundred times. But when she opened her mouth the words didn't come. It happened again throughout the night, and though she made it through she felt embarrassed and subdued—not her usual life-of-the-party self.

A few days later she drove to a friend's place to help them with a balky horse. But she had such a bad headache she could only sit on the fence. Ken was playing a gig out of town, and that night she tried to call him. She needed to tell him about her headache. It wasn't just a headache. The pain was heavy and unrelenting. It felt, well, serious. She didn't reach Ken because she was dialing the wrong number—over and over.

The next day Ken took Tenley to the ER in Missoula where she had an MRI. It showed a tumor in her brain.

Epilog

When Ken was courting Tenley, he came up with a plan he thought would do the trick. He set it up perfectly—a birthday dinner at the Chart House, on the hill overlooking the Willamette River and the whole panoramic view to the east. Their table was at the window, and if you looked down you could see the parking lot. As they were admiring the view a 1974 Triumph TR6 with a big red bow tied around the hood drove in and parked. Tenley had always wanted a TR6, and she said, "Oh look at that. Somebody really knows how to win a girl's heart."

That somebody was Ken and the car was Tenley's birthday present. "I know it was excessive," he says now. "But it was so much fun to make her happy."

The first time I met Tenley she was driving that car near their house in Montana, her hair flying and her gold eyes flashing. The little sports car was her escape, her way out when life was getting her down. She could always go drive the Triumph.

That still worked for a while after she got sick, with Ken driving and Tenley bundled up in the passenger seat, the top down and her scarf flying. But eventually even riding was too much for her. Ken let his towing insurance lapse and hocked his tow truck. There was no time for tow calls or for much of anything other than taking care of Tenley. When someone you love is dying, your world slowly shrinks down to a small point of light that is their remaining self, that place where you might get a smile or a look that tells you they are still in there somewhere.

In the late fall of 2013, a few months after Tenley died, Ken and I sat on his back deck. It was a remarkable day, bright and warm in the sun but with the knife edge of winter ready to stab you from the shadows. We looked at Tenley's garden, brown and sparse after several seasons of neglect, and he told me a story that happened in Ireland. He took Tenley there the autumn after her diagnosis, to visit the county her family was from.

"First of all they drive on the left. And they drive fast," he said. He and Tenley rented a Renault and drove around the narrow Irish roads with stone walls instead of guard rails, so close you could reach out and touch them. In fact, the Renault nearly scraped a wall in a close call involving a big truck in a long row of traffic and an approaching bridge.

But that's not the story Ken wants to tell. The important one is about the Irish pub with cozy rooms upstairs and good strong beer downstairs. He and

140

Tenley sat at the bar, drinking draughts and talking about their day. She was wearing a brightly colored headband scarf to cover her large surgery scar. Ken was looking at her, thinking that she always looked great in a scarf anyway, when two women came in the door. They were also wearing brightly colored scarves tied like Tenley's.

Ken and Tenley looked at the women and then at each other, smiling at the potential for an adventure. A moment later two more women came in with their own bright scarves, and then three more, and it was clear that this was another in the long line of unlikely connections that made life with Tenley mysterious and fun. Soon a dozen or more women in scarves were in the pub, wearing dazzling scarves and pants that nearly matched.

It was a Swedish women's chorus, in Ireland for a concert. In no time Tenley had slipped up to the room and returned with her guitar and her own flashy pants, and the Swedish women—who spoke no English—were singing along with her to *You Are My Sunshine*. As usual, Tenley owned the room.

After Tenley died, Ken sold the TR6. With her gone it was just a car. The house was just a house and the winter days seemed like they'd skip solstice and just keep getting shorter until they disappeared into the dark.

But sometimes when you're not expecting it, Tenley seems to be just around the corner—remembering all the words to Jambalaya, laughing at stories about unwise drivers, hair flying with the top down on the Triumph. Riding shotgun in Ken's heart.

Made in the USA
San Bernardino, CA
07 May 2016